Arizona Diamondbacks 2020

A Baseball Companion

Edited by R.J. Anderson, Craig Goldstein and Bret Sayre

Baseball Prospectus

Craig Brown, Steven Goldman and David Pease, Consultant Editors
Robert Au, Harry Pavlidis and Amy Pircher, Statistics Editors

Copyright © 2020 by DIY Baseball, LLC.
All rights reserved

This book or any part thereof may not be reproduced or transmitted in any form or by any means, electronic or mechanical, including photocopying, recording, or by any information storage and retrieval system, without permission in writing from the publisher.

Limit of Liability/Disclaimer of Warranty: While the publisher and the author have used their best efforts in preparing this book, they make no representations or warranties with respect to the accuracy or completeness of the contents of this book and specifically disclaim any implied warranties of merchantability or fitness for a particular purpose. No warranty may be created or extended by sales representatives or written sales materials. The advice and strategies contained herein may not be suitable for your situation. You should consult with a professional where appropriate. Neither the publisher nor the author shall be liable for any loss of profit or any other commercial damages, including but not limited to special, incidental, consequential, or other damages.

Library of Congress Cataloging-in-Publication Data:
paperback
ISBN-13: 978-1-949332-94-0

Project Credits
Cover Design: Michael Byzewski at Aesthetic Apparatus
Interior Design and Production: Jeff Pease, Dave Pease
Layout: Jeff Pease, Dave Pease

Baseball icon courtesy of Uberux, from https://www.shareicon.net/author/uberux

Ballpark diagram courtesy of Lou Spirito/THIRTY81 Project, https://thirty81project.com/

Manufactured in the United States of America
10 9 8 7 6 5 4 3 2 1

Table of Contents

Statistical Introduction v

Part 1: Team Analysis

Arizona Diamondbacks: Where Are You Going, Where Have You Been? . . 3
    Ginny Searle, Forest Stulting and Matthew Trueblood

Performance Graphs 7

2019 Team Performance 8

2020 Team Projections 9

Team Personnel 10

Chase Field Stats 11

Diamondbacks Team Analysis 13

Part 2: Player Analysis

Diamondbacks Player Analysis 20

Diamondbacks Prospects 101

Part 3: Featured Articles

The Baseball Is Juiced (Again) 117
    Robert Arthur

The Moral Hazard of Playing It Safe 121
    Craig Goldstein

Index of Names 127

Statistical Introduction

Sports are, fundamentally, a blend of athletic endeavor and storytelling. Baseball, like any other sport, tells its stories in so many ways: in the arc of a game from the stands or a season from the box scores, in photos, or even in numbers. At Baseball Prospectus, we understand that statistics don't replace observation or any of baseball's stories, but complement everything else that makes the game so much fun.

What stats help us with is with patterns and precision, variance and value. This book can help you learn things you may not see from watching a game or hundred, whether it's the path of a career over time or the breadth of the entire MLB. We'd also never ask you to choose between our numbers and the experience of viewing a game from the cheap seats or the comfort of your home; our publication combines running the numbers with observations and wisdom from some of the brightest minds we can find. But if you *do* want to learn more about the numbers beyond what's on the backs of player jerseys, let us help explain.

Offense

We've revised our methodology for determining batting value. Long-time readers of the book will notice that we've retired True Average in favor of a new metric: Deserved Runs Created Plus (DRC+). Developed by Jonathan Judge and our stats team, this statistic measures everything a player does at the plate–reaching base, hitting for power, making outs, and moving runners over–and puts it on a scale where 100 equals league-average performance. A DRC+ of 150 is terrific, a DRC+ of 100 is average and a DRC+ of 75 means you better be an excellent defender.

DRC+ also does a better job than any of our previous metrics in taking contextual factors into account. The model adjusts for how the park affects performance, but also for things like the talent of the opposing pitcher, value of different types of batted-ball events, league, temperature and other factors. It's able to describe a player's expected offensive contribution than any other statistic we've found over the years, and also does a better job of predicting future performance as well.

There's a lot more to DRC+'s story, and you can read all about it in greater depth near the end of this book.

Arizona Diamondbacks 2020

The other aspect of run-scoring is baserunning, which we quantify using Baserunning Runs. BRR not only records the value of stolen bases (or getting caught in the act), but also accounts for all the stuff that doesn't show up on the back of a baseball card: a runner's ability to go first to third on a single, or advance on a fly ball.

Defense

Where offensive value is *relatively* easy to identify and understand, defensive value is...not. Over the past dozen years, the sabermetric community has focused mostly on stats based on zone data: a real-live human person records the type of batted ball and estimated landing location, and models are created that give expected outs. From there, you can compare fielders' actual outs to those expected ones. Simple, right?

Unfortunately, zone data has two major issues. First, zone data is recorded by commercial data providers who keep the raw data private unless you pay for it. (All the statistics we build in this book and on our website use public data as inputs.) That hurts our ability to test assumptions or duplicate results. Second, over the years it has become apparent that there's quite a bit of "noise" in zone-based fielding analysis. Sometimes the conclusions drawn from zone data don't hold up to scrutiny, and sometimes the different data provided by different providers don't look anything alike, giving wildly different results. Sometimes the hard-working professional stringers or scorers might unknowingly inflict unconscious bias into the mix: for example good fielders will often be credited with more expected outs despite the data, and ballparks with high press boxes tend to score more line drives than ones with a lower press box.

Enter our Fielding Runs Above Average (FRAA). For most positions, FRAA is built from play-by-play data, which allows us to avoid the subjectivity found in many other fielding metrics. The idea is this: count how many fielding plays are made by a given player and compare that to expected plays for an average fielder at their position (based on pitcher ground ball tendencies and batter handedness). Then we adjust for park and base-out situations.

When it comes to catchers, our methodology is a little different thanks to the laundry list of responsibilities they're tasked with beyond just, well, catching and throwing the ball. By now you've probably heard about "framing" or the art of making umpires more likely to call balls outside the strike zone for strikes. To put this into one tidy number, we incorporate pitch tracking data (for the years it exists) and adjust for important factors like pitcher, umpire, batter and home-field advantage using a mixed-model approach. This grants us a number for how many strikes the catcher is personally adding to (or subtracting from) his pitchers' performance...which we then convert to runs added or lost using linear weights.

Framing is one of the biggest parts of determining catcher value, but we also take into account blocking balls from going past, whether a scorer deems it a passed ball or a wild pitch. We use a similar approach—one that really benefits from the pitch tracking data that tells us what ends up in the dirt and what doesn't. We also include a catcher's ability to prevent stolen bases and how well they field balls in play, and *finally* we come up with our FRAA for catchers.

Pitching

Both pitching and fielding make up the half of baseball that isn't run scoring: run prevention. Separating pitching from fielding is a tough task, and most recent pitching analysis has branched off from Voros McCracken's famous (and controversial) statement, "There is little if any difference among major-league pitchers in their ability to prevent hits on balls hit in the field of play." The research of the analytic community has validated this to some extent, and there are a host of "defense-independent" pitching measures that have been developed to try and extract the effect of the defense behind a hurler from the pitcher's work.

Our solution to this quandary is Deserved Run Average (DRA), our core pitching metric. DRA looks like earned run average (ERA), the tried-and-true pitching stat you've seen on every baseball broadcast or box score from the past century, but it's very different. To start, DRA takes an event-by-event look at what the pitchers does, and adjusts the value of that event based on different environmental factors like park, batter, catcher, umpire, base-out situation, run differential, inning, defense, home field advantage, pitcher role and temperature. That mixed model gives us a pitcher's expected contribution, similar to what we do for our DRC+ model for hitters and FRAA model for catchers. (Oh, and we also consider the pitcher's effect on basestealing and on balls getting past the catcher.)

It's important to note that DRA is set to the scale of runs allowed per nine innings (RA9) instead of ERA, which makes DRA's scale slightly higher than ERA's. The reason for this is because ERA tends to overrate three types of pitchers:

1. Pitchers who play in parks where scorers hand out more errors. Official scorers differ significantly in the frequency at which they assign errors to fielders.
2. Ground-ball pitchers, because a substantial proportion of errors occur on groundballs.
3. Pitchers who aren't very good. Better pitchers often allow fewer unearned runs than bad pitchers, because good pitchers tend to find ways to get out of jams.

Since the last time you picked up an edition of this book, we've also made a few minor changes to DRA to make it better. Recent research into "tunneling"—the act of throwing consecutive pitches that appear similar from a batter's point of view until after the swing decision point–data has given us a new contextual factor to account for in DRA: plate distance. This refers to the distance between successive pitches as they approach the plate, and while it has a smaller effect than factors like velocity or whiff rate, it still can help explain pitcher strikeout rate in our model.

New Pitching Metrics for 2020

We're including a few "new" pitching metrics in the book for the 2020 edition, though unlike last year, these numbers may be a little bit more familiar to those of you who have spent some time investigating baseball statistics.

Fastball Percentage

Our fastball percentage (FB%) statistic measures how frequently a pitcher throws a pitch classified as a "fastball," measured as a percentage of overall pitches thrown. We qualify three types of fastballs:

1. The traditional four-seam fastball;
2. The two-seam fastball or sinker;
3. "Hard cutters," which are pitches that have the movement profile of a cut fastball and are used as the pitcher's primary offering or in place of a more traditional fastball.

For example, a pitcher with a FB% of 67 throws any combination of these three pitches about two-thirds of the time.

Whiff Rate

Everybody loves a swing and a miss, and whiff rate (WHF) measures how frequently pitchers induce a swinging strike. To calculate WHF, we add up all the pitches thrown that ended with a swinging strike, then divide that number by a pitcher's total pitches thrown. Most often, high whiff rates correlate with high strikeout rates (and overall effective pitcher performance).

Called Strike Probability

Called Strike Probability (CSP) is a number that represents the likelihood that all of a pitcher's pitches will be called a strike while controlling for location, pitcher and batter handedness, umpire and count. Here's how it works: on each pitch, our model determines how many times (out of 100) that a similar pitch was called for a strike given those factors mentioned above, and when normalized for each batter's strike zone. Then we average the CSP for all pitches thrown by a pitcher in a season, and that gives us the yearly CSP percentage you see in the stats boxes.

As you might imagine, pitchers with a higher CSP are more likely to work in the zone, where pitchers with a lower CSP are likely locating their pitches outside the normal strike zone, for better or for worse.

Projections

Many of you aren't turning to this book just for a look at what a player has done, but for a look at what a player is going to do: the PECOTA projections. PECOTA, initially developed by Nate Silver (who has moved on to greater fame as a political analyst), consists of three parts:

1. Major-league equivalencies, which use minor-league statistics to project how a player will perform in the major leagues;
2. Baseline forecasts, which use weighted averages and regression to the mean to estimate a player's current true talent level; and
3. Aging curves, which uses the career paths of comparable players to estimate how a player's statistics are likely to change over time.

With all those important things covered, let's take a look at what's in the book this year.

Team Prospectus

Most of this book is composed of team chapters, with one for each of the 30 major-league franchises. On the first page of each chapter, you'll see a box that contains some of the key statistics for each team as well as a very inviting stadium diagram. (You can see an example of this for the Milwaukee Brewers on this very page!)

We start with the team name, their unadjusted 2019 win-loss record, and their divisional ranking. Beneath that are a host of other team statistics. **Pythag** presents an adjusted 2019 winning percentage, calculated by taking runs scored per game (**RS/G**) and runs allowed per game (**RA/G**) for the team, and running them through a version of Bill James' Pythagorean formula that was refined and improved by David Smyth and Brandon Heipp. (The formula is called "Pythagenpat," which is equally fun to type and to say.)

Next up is **DRC+**, described earlier, to indicate the overall hitting ability of the team either above or below league-average. Run prevention on the pitching side is covered by **DRA** (also mentioned earlier) and another metric: Fielding Independent Pitching (**FIP**), which calculates another ERA-like statistic based on strikeouts, walks, and home runs recorded. Defensive Efficiency Rating (**DER**) tells us the percentage of balls in play turned into outs for the team, and is a quick fielding shorthand that rounds out run prevention.

After that, we have several measures related to roster composition, as opposed to on-field performance. **B-Age** and **P-Age** tell us the average age of a team's batters and pitchers, respectively. **Salary** is the combined team payroll for all on-field players, and Doug Pappas' Marginal Dollars per Marginal Win (**M$/MW**) tells us how much money a team spent to earn production above replacement level.

Ending this batch of statistics is the number of disabled list days a team had over the season (**IL Days**) and the amount of salary paid to players on the disabled list (**$ on IL**); this final number is expressed as a percentage of total payroll.

Next to each of these stats, we've listed each team's MLB rank in that category from first to 30th. In this, first always indicates a positive outcome and 30th a negative outcome, except in the case of salary—first is highest.

After the franchise statistics, we share a few items about the team's home ballpark. There's the aforementioned diagram of the park's dimensions (including distances to the outfield wall), a graphic showing the height of the wall from the left-field pole to the right-field pole, and a table showing three-year park factors for the stadium. The park factors are displayed as indexes where 100 is average, 110 means that the park inflates the statistic in question by 10 percent, and 90 means that the park deflates the statistic in question by 10 percent.

On the second page of each team chapter, you'll find three graphs. The first is the **2019 Hit List Ranking**. This shows our Hit List Rank for the team on each day of the 2019 season and is intended to give you a picture of the ups and downs of the team's season. Hit List Rank measures overall team performance and drives the Hit List Power Rankings at the baseballprospectus.com website.

The second graph is **Committed Payroll** and helps you see how the team's payroll has compared to the MLB and divisional average payrolls over time. Payroll figures are current as of January 1, 2020; with so many free agents still unsigned as of this writing, the final 2020 figure will likely be significantly different for many teams. (In the meantime, you can always find the most current data at Baseball Prospectus' Cot's Baseball Contracts page.)

The third graph is **Farm System Ranking** and displays how the Baseball Prospectus prospect team has ranked the organization's farm system since 2007.

After the graphs, we have a **Personnel** section that lists many of the important decision-makers and upper-level field and operations staff members for the franchise, as well as any former Baseball Prospectus staff members who are currently part of the organization. (In very rare circumstances, someone might be on both lists!)

Juan Soto LF

Born: 10/25/98 Age: 21 Bats: L Throws: L
Height: 6'1" Weight: 185 Origin: International Free Agent, 2015

YEAR	TEAM	LVL	AGE	PA	R	2B	3B	HR	RBI	BB	K	SB	CS	AVG/OBP/SLG
2017	NAT	RK	18	27	3	1	1	0	4	2	1	0	0	.320/.370/.440
2017	HAG	A	18	96	15	5	0	3	14	10	8	1	2	.360/.427/.523
2018	HAG	A	19	74	12	5	3	5	24	14	13	2	0	.373/.486/.814
2018	POT	A+	19	73	17	3	1	7	18	11	8	0	1	.371/.466/.790
2018	HAR	AA	19	35	4	2	0	2	10	4	7	1	0	.323/.400/.581
2018	WAS	MLB	19	494	77	25	1	22	70	79	99	5	2	.292/.406/.517
2019	WAS	MLB	20	659	110	32	5	34	110	108	132	12	1	.282/.401/.548
2020	WAS	MLB	21	630	92	30	3	35	102	85	123	5	2	.284/.382/.543

Comparables: Ronald Acuña Jr., Mike Trout, Tony Conigliaro

YEAR	TEAM	LVL	AGE	PA	DRC+	VORP	BABIP	BRR	FRAA	WARP
2017	NAT	RK	18	27	135	1.5	.333	0.0	RF(9): -1.1	0.0
2017	HAG	A	18	96	181	8.0	.373	1.0	RF(19): -1.9, LF(2): -0.3	0.9
2018	HAG	A	19	74	222	14.5	.405	0.3	RF(14): 1.1, CF(2): 0.2	1.2
2018	POT	A+	19	73	260	15.4	.340	1.4	RF(14): 1.0, LF(1): 0.0	1.6
2018	HAR	AA	19	35	113	3.6	.364	0.0	LF(4): 0.6, RF(4): -0.5	0.1
2018	WAS	MLB	19	494	125	40.5	.338	-0.5	LF(114): 2.7	3.0
2019	WAS	MLB	20	659	136	49.0	.312	1.4	LF(150): -0.8	4.9
2020	WAS	MLB	21	630	133	43.6	.310	-0.1	LF 3	4.8

Position Players

After all that information and a thoughtful bylined essay covering each team, we present our player comments. These are also bylined, but due to frequent franchise shifts during the offseason, our bylines are more a rough guide than a perfect accounting of who wrote what.

Each player is listed with the major-league team that employed him as of early January 2020. If a player changed teams after that point via free agency, trade, or any other method, you'll be able to find them in the chapter for their previous squad.

As an example, take a look at the player comment for Nationals outfielder Juan Soto: the stat block that accompanies his written comment is at the top of this page. First we cover biographical information (age is as of June 30, 2020) before moving onto the stats themselves. Our statistic columns include standard identifying information like **YEAR**, **TEAM**, **LVL** (level of affiliated play) and **AGE** before getting into the numbers. Next, we provide raw, untranslated numbers like you might find on the back of your dad's baseball cards: **PA** (plate appearances), **R** (runs), **2B** (doubles), **3B** (triples), **HR** (home runs), **RBI** (runs batted in), **BB** (walks), **K** (strikeouts), **SB** (stolen bases) and **CS** (caught stealing).

Next, we have unadjusted "slash" statistics: **AVG** (batting average), **OBP** (on-base percentage) and **SLG** (slugging percentage). Following the slash line is **DRC+** (Deserved Runs Created Plus), which we described earlier as total offensive expected contribution compared to the league average.

One of our oldest active metrics, **VORP** (Value Over Replacement Player), considers offensive production, position and plate appearances. In essence, it is the number of runs contributed beyond what a replacement-level player at the same position would contribute if given the same percentage of team plate appearances. VORP does not consider the quality of a player's defense.

BABIP (batting average on balls in play) tells us how often a ball in play fell for a hit, and can help us identify whether a batter may have been lucky or not…but note that high BABIPs also tend to follow the great hitters of our time, as well as speedy singles hitters who put the ball on the ground.

The next item is **BRR** (Baserunning Runs), which covers all of a player's baserunning accomplishments including (but not limited to) swiped bags and failed attempts. Next is **FRAA** (Fielding Runs Above Average), which also includes the number of games previously played at each position noted in parentheses. Multi-position players have only their two most frequent positions listed here, but their total FRAA number reflects all positions played.

Our last column here is **WARP** (Wins Above Replacement Player). WARP estimates the total value of a player, which means for hitters it takes into account hitting runs above average (calculated using the DRC+ model), BRR and FRAA. Then, it makes an adjustment for positions played and gives the player a credit for plate appearances based upon the difference between "replacement level"—which is derived from the quality of players added to a team's roster after the start of the season–and the league average.

The final line just below the stats box is **PECOTA** data, which is discussed further in a following section.

Catchers

Catchers are a special breed, and thus they have earned their own separate box which displays some of the defensive metrics that we've built just for them. As an example, let's check out J.T. Realmuto.

The **YEAR** and **TEAM** columns match what you'd find in the other stat box. **P. COUNT** indicates the number of pitches thrown while the catcher was behind the plate, including swinging strikes, fouls and balls in play. **FRM RUNS** is the total run value the catcher provided (or cost) his team by influencing the umpire to call strikes where other catchers did not. **BLK RUNS** expresses the total run value above or below average for the catcher's ability to prevent wild pitches and passed balls. **THRW RUNS** is calculated using a similar model as the previous two statistics, and it measures a catcher's ability to throw out basestealers but also to dissuade them from testing his arm in the first place. It takes into account factors like the pitcher (including his delivery and pickoff move) and baserunner (who could be as fast as Billy Hamilton or as slow as Yonder Alonso). **TOT RUNS** is the sum of all of the previous three statistics.

Justin Verlander   RHP
Born: 02/20/83   Age: 37   Bats: R   Throws: R
Height: 6'5"   Weight: 225   Origin: Round 1, 2004 Draft (#2 overall)

YEAR	TEAM	LVL	AGE	W	L	SV	G	GS	IP	H	HR	BB/9	K/9	K	GB%	BABIP
2017	DET	MLB	34	10	8	0	28	28	172	153	23	3.5	9.2	176	34%	.283
2017	HOU	MLB	34	5	0	0	5	5	34	17	4	1.3	11.4	43	32%	.194
2018	HOU	MLB	35	16	9	0	34	34	214	156	28	1.6	12.2	290	31%	.272
2019	HOU	MLB	36	21	6	0	34	34	223	137	36	1.7	12.1	300	36%	.219
2020	HOU	MLB	37	15	6	0	29	29	184	138	28	2.3	12.1	248	35%	.274

Comparables: Zack Greinke, A.J. Burnett, Aníbal Sánchez

YEAR	TEAM	LVL	AGE	WHIP	ERA	DRA	WARP	MPH	FB%	WHF	CSP
2017	DET	MLB	34	1.28	3.82	4.03	3.0	97.7	58	11	47.8
2017	HOU	MLB	34	0.65	1.06	3.08	0.9	97.5	59.6	15.1	49.9
2018	HOU	MLB	35	0.90	2.52	2.33	7.3	97.5	61.2	16.2	51.6
2019	HOU	MLB	36	0.80	2.58	2.51	7.9	96.8	49.9	17.5	48.3
2020	HOU	MLB	37	1.01	2.75	2.95	5.3	95.8	54.6	15.1	48.2

Pitchers

Let's give our pitchers a turn, using 2019 AL Cy Young winner Justin Verlander as our example. Take a look at his stat block: the first line and the **YEAR**, **TEAM**, **LVL** and **AGE** columns are the same as in the position player example earlier.

Here too, we have a series of columns that display raw, unadjusted statistics compiled by the pitcher over the course of a season: **W** (wins), **L** (losses), **SV** (saves), **G** (games pitched), **GS** (games started), **IP** (innings pitched), **H** (hits allowed) and **HR** (home runs allowed). Next we have two statistics that are rates: **BB/9** (walks per nine innings) and **K/9** (strikeouts per nine innings), before returning to the unadjusted K (strikeouts).

Next up is **GB%** (ground ball percentage), which is the percentage of all batted balls that were hit on the ground, including both outs and hits. Remember, this is based on observational data and subject to human error, so please approach this with a healthy dose of skepticism.

BABIP (batting average on balls in play) is calculated using the same methodology as it is for position players, but it often tells us more about a pitcher than it does a hitter. With pitchers, a high BABIP is often due to poor defense or bad luck, and can often be an indicator of potential rebound, and a low BABIP may be cause to expect performance regression. (A typical league-average BABIP is close to .290-.300.)

The metrics **WHIP** (walks plus hits per inning pitched) and **ERA** (earned run average) are old standbys: WHIP measures walks and hits allowed on a per-inning basis, while ERA measures earned runs on a nine-inning basis. Neither of these stats are translated or adjusted.

DRA (Deserved Run Average) was described at length earlier, and measures how many runs the pitcher "deserved" to allow per nine innings. Please note that since we lack all the data points that would make for a "real" DRA for minor-league events, the DRA displayed for minor league partial-seasons is based off of different data. (That data is a modified version of our cFIP metric, which you can find more information about on our website.)

Just like with hitters, **WARP** (Wins Above Replacement Player) is a total value metric that puts pitchers of all stripes on the same scale as position players. We use DRA as the primary input for our calculation of WARP. You might notice that relief pitchers (due to their limited innings) may have a lower WARP than you were expecting or than you might see in other WARP-like metrics. WARP does not take leverage into account, just the actions a pitcher performs and the expected value of those actions...which ends up judging high-leverage relief pitchers differently than you might imagine given their prestige and market value.

MPH gives you the pitcher's 95th percentile velocity for the noted season, in order to give you an idea of what the *peak* fastball velocity a pitcher possesses. Since this comes from our pitch-tracking data, it is not publicly available for minor-league pitchers.

Finally, we display the three new pitching metrics we described earlier. **FB%** (fastball percentage) gives you the percentage of fastballs thrown out of all pitches. **WHF** (whiff rate) tells you the percentage of swinging strikes induced out of all pitches. **CSP** (called strike probability) expresses the likelihood of all pitches thrown to result in a called strike, after controlling for factors like handedness, umpire, pitch type, count and location.

PECOTA

All players have PECOTA projections for 2020, as well as a set of other numbers that describe the performance of comparable players according to PECOTA. All projections for 2020 are for the player at the date we went to press in early January and are projected into the league and park context as indicated by the team abbreviation. (Note that players at very low levels of the minors are too unpredictable to assess using these numbers.) All PECOTA projected statistics represent a player's projected major-league performance.

Below the projections are the player's three highest-scoring comparable players as determined by PECOTA. All comparables represent a snapshot of how the listed player was performing at the same age as the current player, so if a

23-year-old pitcher is compared to Bartolo Colón, he's actually being compared to a 23-year-old Colón, not the version that pitched for the Rangers in 2018, nor to Colón's career as a whole.

A few points about pitcher projections. First, we aren't yet projecting peak velocity, so that column will be blank in the PECOTA lines. Second, projecting DRA is trickier than evaluating past performance, because it is unclear how deserving each pitcher will be of his anticipated outcomes. However, we know that another DRA-related statistic–contextual FIP or cFIP–estimates future run scoring very well. So for PECOTA, the projected DRA figures you see are based on the past cFIPs generated by the pitcher and comparable players over time, along with the other factors described above.

Lineouts

In each chapter's Lineouts section, you'll find abbreviated text comments, as well as all the same information you'd find in our full player comments. The only difference is that we limit the stats boxes in this section to only including the 2019 information for each player.

Managers

After all those wonderful team chapters, we've got statistics for each big-league manager, all of whom are organized by alphabetical order. Here you'll find a block including an extraordinary amount of information collected from each manager's entire career. For more information on the acronyms and what they mean, please visit the Glossary at www.baseballprospectus.com.

There is one important metric that we'd like to call attention to, and you'll find it next to each manager's name: **wRM+** (weighted reliever management plus). Developed by Rob Arthur and Rian Watt, wRM+ investigates how good a manager is at using their best relievers during the moments of highest leverage, using both our proprietary DRA metric as well as Leverage Index. wRM+ is scaled to a league average of 100, and a wRM+ of 105 indicates that relievers were used approximately five percent "better" than average. On the other hand, a wRM+ of 95 would tell us the team used its relievers five percent "worse" than the average team.

While wRM+ does not have an extremely strong correlation with a manager, it is statistically significant; this means that a manager is not *entirely* responsible for a team's wRM+, but does have some effect on that number.

PECOTA Leaderboards

If you're familiar with PECOTA, then you'll have noticed that the projection system often appears bullish on players coming off a bad year and bearish on players coming off a good year. (This is because the system weights several previous seasons, not just the most recent one.) In addition, we publish the 50th

Arizona Diamondbacks 2020

percentile projections for each player–which is smack in the middle of the range of projected production—which tends to mean PECOTA stat lines don't often have extreme results like 40 home runs or 250 strikeouts in a given season. In essence, PECOTA doesn't project very many extreme seasons.

At the end of the book, we've ranked the top players at each position based on their PECOTA projections. This might help you visualize just how a given player's projection compares to that of their peers, so that even if a dramatic stat line isn't projected, you can still imagine how they stack up against the rest of the league.

Part 1: Team Analysis

Arizona Diamondbacks: Where Are You Going, Where Have You Been?

Ginny Searle, Forest Stulting and Matthew Trueblood

2019: What Went Right?
Let's kick things off with a game: Aside from the $24 million promised to Houston as part of the Zack Greinke deal, the Diamondbacks have five payroll commitments for 2020 and beyond. Can you name them?

You might remember the Snakes are still linked to Yasmany Tomás for one more season—the six-year deal Tomás signed as a free agent out of his native Cuba will expire after next season. That one's not something that went "right," but everyone is past expecting a return on that contract and the light at the end of the tunnel is now in view. Ketel Marte signed a five-year, $24 million deal in March ahead of his breakout season, signing away his first free agent season and giving the D'backs two more options on top of that. So that's better than the Tomás contract, especially given Marte's apparent emergence as an All-Star—a stress reaction in his lower back ended his season at 144 games, 32 home runs and a .981 OPS with a team-high 4.5 WARP—and youth (he's entering his age-26 season). Whether in the outfield or the infield, Marte is a big part of Arizona's plans moving forward.

The third contract belongs to Eduardo Escobar, a three-year, $21 million extension inked in October 2018. I feel confident if I gave you five guesses, you wouldn't have pegged Escobar as the NL triples leader, and even in 2019's home run environment 35 dingers was nothing to sneeze at. All told, he was worth 3.3 WARP and been a reliable—if below-average—defender at third, also tossing in a few hundred innings at second. Another significant piece under contract, if one who has not performed as well as the team might have dreamed, is Merrill Kelley. After spending four seasons in Korea after a tepid minor league stint, Kelley was basically league-average in his MLB debut campaign, and right in line with expectations—even at a DRA- of 101, the D'backs would likely pick up his 2021 extension ($4.25 million, $500k buyout) if next year Kelley repeated his 177 2/3 innings and 4.31 ERA from 2019.

We've arrived at our last contracted Snake, Mike Leake. The soft-tossing righty is owed $16 million for 2020 plus a $5 million buyout of a 2021 option, but the Mariners are covering $14 million of that $20 million (and part of that is being paid by the Cardinals). Leake is inexpensive, is the point. If he can continue being a league-average starter this season, there's something to be said for having a settled rotation.

A settled rotation the Diamondbacks certainly have, to whatever degree such a thing can exist in baseball. The Greinke trade left them without an ace, at least momentarily. While Robbie Ray can do a passable imitation—since 2017 he has tossed 454 innings with a 3.69 ERA and compiled 8.6 WARP—the addition of Madison Bumgarner gives them a pitcher who has played that role in the past, even if he is now a few years removed from his peak. Luke Weaver has flashed ace potential when healthy, striking out 9.7 batters per nine while walking just two—in just 64 2/3 innings he has 1.5 WARP, and his recent return gives hope he'll be fully healthy for next year. Then there's Alex Young, who came out of the ether to become a reliable rotation piece in the season's second half (3.27 ERA; though both DRA and a 7.9 K/9 suggest some regression is coming, the lefty has still been well above average). Finally, Zac Gallen has continued to impress since the challenge trade that saw Jazz Chisholm sent to the Marlins)—a sub-3.00 ERA might not carry to next season, but he still looks like a solid number-two starter and is just 24. Add in Leake and that's six starters for five slots, but excesses of depth usually have a way of solving themselves.

The positives begin to run dry outside of those strengths. Archie Bradley (60 IP, 3.65 ERA) and Andrew Chafin (51 1/3 IP, 3.86 ERA) have been fine in the bullpen, and in their few months with the team both Kevin Ginkey and Stefan Crichton made strong cases for themselves. Nick Ahmed has continued to be an excellent defender, and this year finally approached average at the plate, giving him a career-high 3.5 WARP. Carson Kelly looks like an everyday catcher—wow, does that Paul Goldschmidt trade look good for this front office right now.

2019: What Went Wrong?

The bullpen. In 2018, T.J. McFarland had a 2.00 ERA across 72 innings, but DRA was unmoved and assigned him a 4.72 mark. A year later, McFarland's ERA was 4.94 and his DRA nearly two runs beyond that. Zack Godley made nine starts and twice that many appearances in relief and was ineffective in both before being designated for assignment in August. Greg Holland, signed on a one-year free agent deal, wasn't exactly bad, but the team was dreaming of his 0.66 ERA from the second half of 2018 rather than a near-rehash of his 4.66 mark for the full season. DRA liked Matt Andriese, but a 4.86 ERA over nearly 70 innings led to a trade to the Angels. Yoshihisa Hirano was almost exactly league average in both of his two MLB seasons and decamped as a free agent. It's not certain that free agent additions Héctor Rondón and Junior Guerra will entirely solve the problem.

In some ways, the bullpen is a microcosm of the overall problem in Arizona: It's not even a "stars-and-scrubs" issue, it's more, "(not-stars)-and-scrubs." That might seem unfair to a team that wasn't eliminated until the 23rd of September and had the NL's fifth-best run differential but consider that beyond the six position players who produced at least 2.0 WARP, there wasn't a single player who crested 1.0 wins. Wilmer Flores was functional when healthy but his option wasn't picked up. The extended time both he and Jake Lamb spent on the shelf exposed a lack of depth on the positional side. Ildemaro Vargas and Tim Locastro were both on the field as much as Lamb. There's also the larger issue that Lamb, injured for most of the last two campaigns, has simply not been good in either of them.

Another ailment that altered the course of the D'backs' season: The horrific leg injury Steven Souza Jr. suffered just before the season, costing him the year and his original models of a bunch of tendons. Jarrod Dyson and Adam Jones both under-performed in his stead, though the combined 970 plate appearances afforded to the two was probably more than should have been asked of them at this point in their careers. David Peralta still put up 2.0 WARP (his third consecutive year crossing that threshold) across the 99 games persistent shoulder injuries did not prevent him from playing, but his 96 DRC+ represented a significant step back, and with his salary likely approaching $10 million in his final year of arbitration it is unclear what can be expected of him.

The team gave Josh Rojas 157 plate appearances after acquiring him in the Greinke deal and he had just a 61 DRC+. In a larger sense, both his quick promotion and the playing time given to Dyson and Jones point to the same issues: this team doesn't have much positional depth, and it's not clear that the internal options to fill in the gaps are ready. That's not the worst problem in the world, which might not be surprising for a team that dealt an ace still at his peak and remained in contention until the season's last week, and it's one that appears, at least, easily solvable. —*Ginny Searle*

Prospect Outlook

The Diamondbacks have an intriguing farm system. However, most of their top-tier talent lies in the low minors, leaving them few options from within to impact the big-league club next year. **Jon Duplantier** has already made his debut and it's hard to see him having a huge impact this year. Before the emergence of catcher Carson Kelly, **Daulton Varsho's** future seemed assured. Varsho has gotten work at other positions, but not enough to be confident he will get regular at-bats outside of playing behind the dish. But Varsho is the D'backs prospect most likely to have an impact in the majors if given a chance, with his plus speed and hit tool. The only other two options Arizona has that could make a difference in Phoenix are 1B/LF **Seth Beer** and RHP **J.B. Bukauskas**, both of whom came over in the Zack Greinke trade, but neither are sure-fire bets. Beer's main pull is his powerful left-handed stroke, but defensively he doesn't have a true spot to call home. Bukauskas, on the other hand, took a step back this year.

Going forward, though, Arizona will have plenty of options via the depth they currently have in the low minors. It all starts with outfielder **Kristian Robinson**. It doesn't get better than a true five-tool center fielder. Two other outfielders who will get to the Show before Robinson are **Alek Thomas** and **Dominic Fletcher**, both players with above-average gloves and plus hit tools that will speed up their ETA. Even after trading away Jazz Chisholm, the D'backs still have one of the better-fielding, if not the best-fielding, shortstops in all of the minors in **Geraldo Perdomo**. There isn't a play this kid can't make in the field and his approach at the plate is extremely advanced. On the bump, a trio of young right-handers—**Levi Kelly**, **Matt Tabor** and **Luis Frias**—highlight a crop of potential impact pitchers at the big-league level. Frias is the one everybody should keep their eyes on. —*Forest Stulting*

2020 Outlook

The Diamondbacks continue to reload and reshuffle without rebuilding. These days, many teams have shifted their focus from the near-term to the long-term. The Arizona front office lives in the undervalued territory in between; they plan for the medium-term future. Bumgarner fortified their rotation and raised its floor handsomely. Extending Peralta through 2022 and signing Kole Calhoun to a two-year deal gave them similar stability and certitude in the outfield corners, even if each player has obvious warts.

Those moves still left an opening for a final, crystallizing addition, though. The roster needed something, or someone, to simultaneously catalyze it and lend it coherence. Ketel Marte's versatility gave Hazen the flexibility to explore several options, and when he finally pounced, he found a dynamic and high-upside target. Starling Marte will anchor the outfield defense, take pressure off Christian Walker to provide the only purely right-handed thump in the lineup, and raise the ceiling for the club. He doesn't make the Diamondbacks likely Dodger-beaters, but he does make the team's emphasis on depth and risk aversion in other moves much more rational. —*Matthew Trueblood*

Performance Graphs

2019 Hit List Ranking

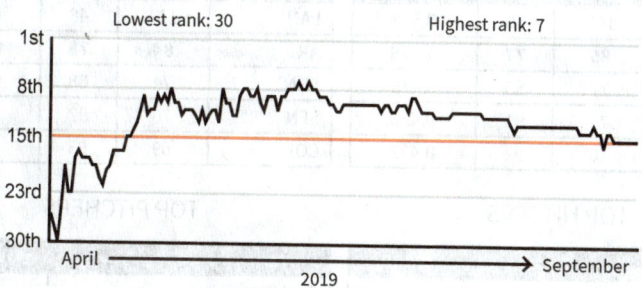

Committed Payroll (in millions)

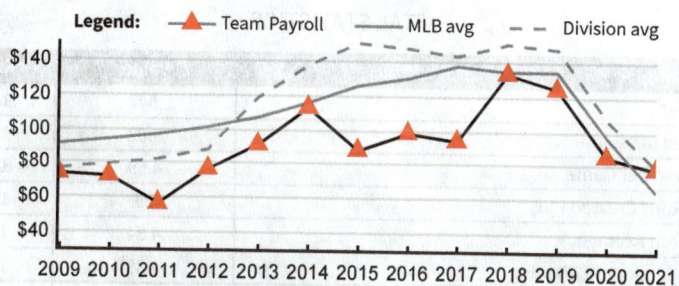

Farm System Ranking

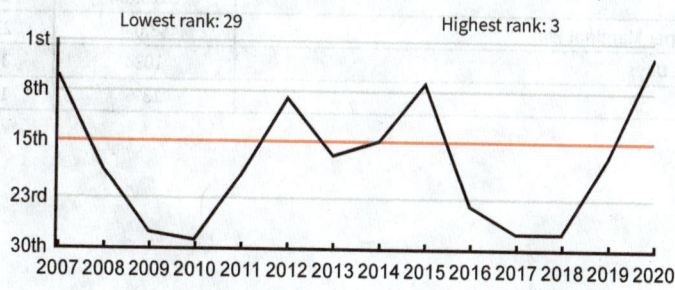

2019 Team Performance

ACTUAL STANDINGS

Team	W	L	Pct
LAN	106	56	0.654
ARI	**85**	**77**	**0.525**
SFN	77	85	0.475
COL	71	91	0.438
SDN	70	92	0.432

THIRD-ORDER STANDINGS

Team	W	L	Pct
LAN	114	48	0.702
ARI	**84**	**78**	**0.516**
SDN	74	88	0.454
SFN	70	92	0.431
COL	69	93	0.429

TOP HITTERS

Player	WARP
Ketel Marte	4.5
Eduardo Escobar	3.3
Nick Ahmed	3.2

TOP PITCHERS

Player	WARP
Zack Greinke	4.3
Robbie Ray	3.2
Merrill Kelly	1.6

VITAL STATISTICS

Statistic Name	Value	Rank
Pythagenpat	.542	12th
Runs Scored per Game	5.02	10th
Runs Allowed per Game	4.59	12th
Deserved Runs Created Plus	95	16th
Deserved Run Average	4.84	14th
Fielding Independent Pitching	4.35	14th
Defensive Efficiency Rating	.705	13th
Batter Age	28.8	24th
Pitcher Age	28.6	19th
Salary	$123.8M	16th
Marginal $ per Marginal Win	$3.0M	22nd
Injured List Days	1034	13th
$ on IL	13%	10th

2020 Team Projections

PROJECTED STANDINGS

Team	W	L	Pct	+/-
LAN	102.5	59.5	0.633	-4
SDN	79.3	82.7	0.490	9
ARI	**78.9**	**83.1**	**0.487**	**-6**
COL	76.6	85.4	0.473	6
SFN	68.4	93.6	0.422	-9

TOP PROJECTED HITTERS

Player	WARP
Starling Marte	3.4
Ketel Marte	3.3
Carson Kelly	2.3

TOP PROJECTED PITCHERS

Player	WARP
Madison Bumgarner	3.8
Zac Gallen	2.9
Robbie Ray	2.4

FARM SYSTEM REPORT

Top Prospect	Number of Top 101 Prospects
Kristian Robinson, #16	4

KEY DEDUCTIONS

Player	WARP
Taijuan Walker	1.0
Alex Avila	0.7
Wilmer Flores	0.7
Matt Andriese	0.7
Yoshihisa Hirano	0.3
Jarrod Dyson	0.2
Steven Souza Jr.	0.1
T.J. McFarland	-0.1

KEY ADDITIONS

Player	WARP
Madison Bumgarner	3.8
Starling Marte	3.4
Kole Calhoun	1.1
Wyatt Mathisen	0.8
Héctor Rondón	0.7
Andy Young	0.2
Seth Beer	0.2
Junior Guerra	0.2
Stephen Vogt	0.1
Daulton Varsho	0.1

Team Personnel

President & Chief Executive Officer
Derrick Hall

Executive Vice President & General Manager
Mike Hazen

Sr. Vice President & Assistant General Manager
Jared Porter

Sr. Vice President & Assistant General Manager
Amiel Sawdaye

Manager
Torey Lovullo

BP Alumni
Hudson Belinsky
Tucker Blair
Jason Parks

Chase Field Stats

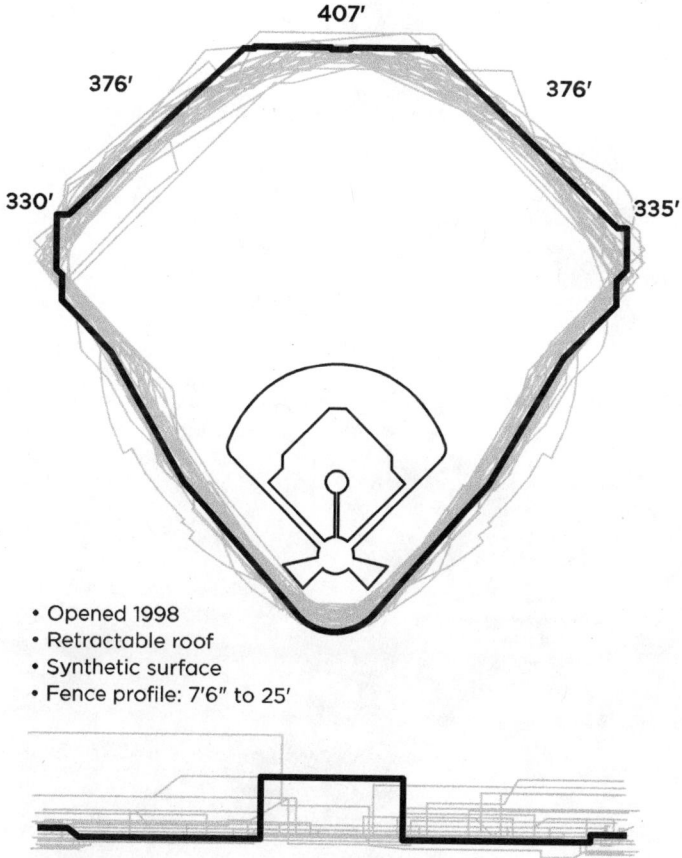

- Opened 1998
- Retractable roof
- Synthetic surface
- Fence profile: 7'6" to 25'

Three-Year Park Factors

Runs	Runs/RH	Runs/LH	HR/RH	HR/LH
103	102	107	100	101

Diamondbacks Team Analysis

Watching the Washington Nationals win the World Series must have been a lonely feeling for the Arizona Diamondbacks. No, the D-backs didn't lose to the Nats in the NLCS—the Snakes didn't even make the playoffs. But there were sure a lot of familiar faces on the field as the 2019 season came to its close. Many of those faces were celebrating while a few hung their heads in improbable defeat. For D-backs fans, watching the World Series seemed like a kind of Bizzaro World straight out of a Seinfeld episode. Minus the funny stuff, obviously.

Long-time Diamondback Daniel Hudson threw that final strike for the Nationals while Game 7 starter Max Scherzer was a Diamondbacks draftee and debuted in the desert. Former rotation stalwart Patrick Corbin provided three innings of important relief and 2010 draftee Adam Eaton got on base twice and scored a run, while a homegrown Gerardo Parra cheered on from the bench. On the losing side, Zack Greinke pitched marvelously for the Astros following his midseason trade to Houston and former D-backs reliever Will Harris played a pivotal role as he surrendered a lead that would not be regathered. Even the coaches got in on the action—Chip Hale, Alex Cintrón and Henry Blanco were all either former Diamondbacks players and/or coaches.

Arizona wasn't the only franchise to have former players on the field, of course, but the sheer bulk of them underscores a trend that's been persistent for much of the team's short history: The organization has been rather good at procuring talent. The trouble has come from the franchise's inability to capitalize on and/or retain the talent they've acquired.

A public spat ran its course before Justin Upton was shipped out of town, the team surrendered Scherzer before he was really given a chance to become Mad Max, first-round pick Trevor Bauer didn't mesh and was traded abruptly, the late Tyler Skaggs was traded for and then dealt before he could gain much traction (for Mark Trumbo, no less) and first-overall pick Dansby Swanson was sent packing along with homespun talent Ender Inciarte in what is probably baseball's worst trade of the last five years (see: Miller, Shelby). The returns weren't always bad and there were plenty of other trades that were just fine. The results from *these* transactions, however, indicate that the Diamondbacks frequently forwent premium production from the talent they collected, and in an attempt to hang on to relevance, often pushing their chips in further to their own detriment.

Arizona Diamondbacks 2020

At the conclusion of the 2018 season, General Manager Mike Hazen faced a familiar line of questioning. Patrick Corbin and A.J. Pollock were set to hit free agency. Paul Goldschmidt was in the final year of his deal and hadn't signed a long-term extension. Zack Greinke was eating nearly a third of the team's payroll. Were the Diamondbacks going to join several other clubs in tearing down their roster and rebuild? Their history of selling short made rebuilding sound somewhat appealing. Wipe the slate clean, start over. The historic value left on the table wasn't Hazen's doing, but the idea was en vogue across baseball.

Instead, the Diamondbacks bucked the trend and didn't go down the path of a full rebuild simply because they didn't have to.

When Hazen took over the role of GM in October of 2016, he had a clear mission: build a more sustainable winner. When asked about his perception of the organization's collection of talent prior to taking the job, Hazen summarized the situation neatly.

> "Looking back on it, I think it's hard to tell what you really have. You can evaluate things from afar, but it's hard to know without really being involved on the day-to-day how much talent you have. I think the general consensus was (that) the major league team was fairly talented and underperformed in 2016. They had spent quite a few of their resources to put that team together. The Shelby Miller trade being one where they had traded a number of young players in that deal. And then, the farm system—same. Using young players to make trades like that to bolster the major-league team, I just think that's naturally going to impact your general level of depth. I think a lot of our talent was aggregated at the major-league level and I think shared the responsibility for us getting to the playoffs in 2017. I think when we came in we knew and were told that building something sustainable from the ground level up was important and we have certainly spent a lot of our time doing that over the last three years."

Those three years have been remarkably focused. When other teams were lining up to zig (rebuild), the Diamondbacks zagged (re-tooled). And rather than make a familiar mistake in trying to recapture the magic, the team made bold moves in trading Goldschmidt and Greinke while making no major push (at least publicly) to re-sign the players they had made qualifying offers to in Corbin and Pollock. The trade returns were surprisingly good considering Goldschmidt had just one year left on his deal and Greinke was still owed a massive sum as an aging pitcher with diminished stuff. The QOs turned into extra draft picks as the D-backs boasted seven selections in the top 75 last June and nine inside the top 100. Those subtractions also freed up plenty of capital that could be reinvested.

That sounds an awful lot like a team that's trying to tank, but the Diamondbacks never saw it that way. The organization plays in a market full of transplants, and given the franchise's relative youth, there's no storied history to pull generational fans into the fold. Competing in earnest on the diamond year after year is the only way to keep the team relevant in their own home territory, something other franchises don't have to worry about so acutely. And compete they did in 2019—without many of the household names—to the tune of an 85-win season, one in which they remained in the playoff hunt until the final two weeks.

Recapturing organizational value while simultaneously trying to win is a difficult balance to strike, but that's a line that Hazen and his deputies continued to walk in 2019.

> "Well, when we were making most of our deals, one of the things we kept reminding ourselves was, because we were trying to compete, was we were trying to both satisfy the current and future in most deals. So we didn't end up doing a lot of deals that returned lower A-ball players. Maybe we yielded some upside in that thought process, but we tried to get younger as much as we could, but close to the big leagues in order to bring back guys that could help our major league team. We haven't gotten back to the playoffs, but we have tried to remain competitive because we thought that was important. So, when we were making a lot of these deals, that was one of the things we focused on was trying to both improve ourselves in the long term and also improve ourselves in the short term."

Rather than make a play for the deep rebuild, the team's biggest trades all brought back players that were either big leaguers or right on the cusp of their debuts. Goldschmidt turned into Luke Weaver and Carson Kelly. Greinke turned into Seth Beer, Corbin Martin, J.B. Bukauskas and Josh Rojas. They even flipped top prospect Jazz Chisholm for Zac Gallen. Kelly, Weaver, Gallen and Rojas have already paid dividends. Beer and Bukauskas are nearly ready and when Martin's elbow is healed, he'll factor heavily into the rotation discussion. None of those players compare to a Goldschmidt or a Greinke right now in terms of perennial value, but they sure can help bolster a roster for pennies on the dollar.

While the organization could spend more money, Hazen has done a tremendous job of working within his constraints to put a winner on the field despite subtracting some marquee talent. Because, even after those subtractions, there was still an enviable amount of talent to draw from. Things have to break right, but it helps when Ketel Marte signs a long-term extension and plays like an MVP candidate. It helps when Eduardo Escobar inks a team-friendly deal and has his best season while wearing Sedona Red. It helps when a young starter with six years of team control (Gallen) is made available by the Marlins. It helps when Carson Kelly takes full advantage of real, legitimate playing time and becomes the type of player he was forecast to be three or four years ago. Each of these moves—and dozens of others—are still bets at the end of the day. But those bets are working out consistently in Hazen's favor.

While formalizing important deals with Marte and Escobar, and acquiring about half a dozen current and future big league pieces, Hazen's organization has also gotten their hands on an intriguing mashup of amateur-turned-pro talent. The Diamondbacks have scored big over the past three drafts, finding talents like Daulton Varsho, Alek Thomas and Corbin Carroll. They've supplemented the domestic draftees with guys like Kristian Robinson, Liover Peguero, Wilderd Patino and Jeferson Espinal. The organization has also seen inherited international players like Geraldo Perdomo and Luis Frias take big steps forward. A minor-league system that was very recently near or at the bottom of the heap is now in the discussion for a top-five system in baseball, something Hazen and his staff deserve the lion's share of the credit for.

⚾ ⚾ ⚾

The Diamondbacks were able to avoid the rebuild because they still had quality contributors in place at the major-league level, an improving farm system established, a boatload of draft picks on the horizon, and more international bonus money to play with. They have proven capable of cashing in some their current chips for future ones while developing the ones they held onto. They played their cards right with impending free agents and received additional draft picks. They moved key pieces and got back enough talent to justify the moves. The easy perception is that, under Hazen's direction, the organization has made real progress in adding talent, value and depth to a system that didn't have nearly as much of those things just a few years ago. When asked if he feels accomplished to any degree in this work, Hazen's response was binary and straightforward.

> "No, not really. I think our job is, at a basic level, to be improving the talent of our organization. I think that's an expectation of all of the 30 teams. So saying that you're doing that to any degree is, I think, just a prerequisite for the job. I think how teams turn that into wins at the major league level is the separator. We haven't done that to a good enough degree to make the playoffs and we want to compete next year. We don't know what next year is going to bring."

It's a results-oriented business, after all. And it's unclear if the D-backs are going to be able to turn a healthy portion of their newfound talent into major league wins. That's something that previous Diamondbacks regimes have often failed to do. Fans of the team have been down this road before and will again approach the idea of the franchise building serious momentum with a healthy dose of skepticism. But if the current indicators are to be trusted at all, it appears that brighter days are ahead. Whether they come in 2020 or not is debatable. But the long-term forecast is more encouraging than it has been in quite some time.

—*Jeff Wiser is an author of Baseball Prospectus.*

Part 2: Player Analysis

PLAYER COMMENTS WITH GRAPHS

Nick Ahmed SS
Born: 03/15/90 Age: 30 Bats: R Throws: R
Height: 6'2" Weight: 195 Origin: Round 2, 2011 Draft (#85 overall)

YEAR	TEAM	LVL	AGE	PA	R	2B	3B	HR	RBI	BB	K	SB	CS	AVG/OBP/SLG
2017	ARI	MLB	27	178	24	8	1	6	21	10	39	3	4	.251/.298/.419
2018	ARI	MLB	28	564	61	33	5	16	70	40	109	5	4	.234/.290/.411
2019	ARI	MLB	29	625	79	33	6	19	82	52	113	8	2	.254/.316/.437
2020	ARI	MLB	30	630	60	29	4	16	67	47	124	8	5	.224/.286/.373

Comparables: Didi Gregorius, Greg Gagne, Dale Berra

UrbanDictionary.com eloquently defines the phrase "Get you a man who can do both" as "To be in a relationship when your boyfriend is classy, kind, and deep but thug'n it at the same time." For years, the Diamondbacks couldn't get that phrase out of their heads in regards to their six spot—staring longingly at other shortstops who could do both, while they were stuck with their nice guy without an ounce of "bad boy" in his body. Ahmed heard this and underwent a transformation akin to DJ Qualls in "The New Guy," finally pairing his usual sterling defense with palatable offensive production. Nobody will ever confuse Ahmed with Francisco Lindor or Young Thug, but a shortstop who can do both makes you reconsider the relationship altogether instead of saying "on to the next one."

YEAR	TEAM	LVL	AGE	PA	DRC+	VORP	BABIP	BRR	FRAA	WARP
2017	ARI	MLB	27	178	80	1.5	.295	-0.8	SS(48): 3.9	0.7
2018	ARI	MLB	28	564	89	17.5	.265	-0.4	SS(148): 15.1	3.3
2019	ARI	MLB	29	625	93	24.4	.280	2.4	SS(158): 6.0	3.2
2020	ARI	MLB	30	630	77	5.5	.259	0.7	SS 10	1.6

Nick Ahmed, continued

Batted Ball Distribution

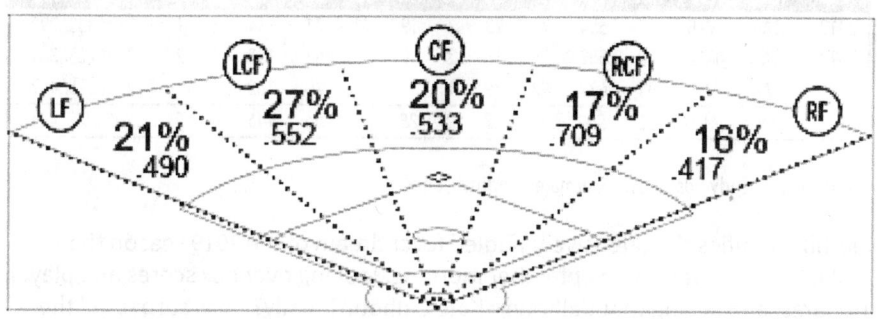

Strike Zone vs LHP **Strike Zone vs RHP**

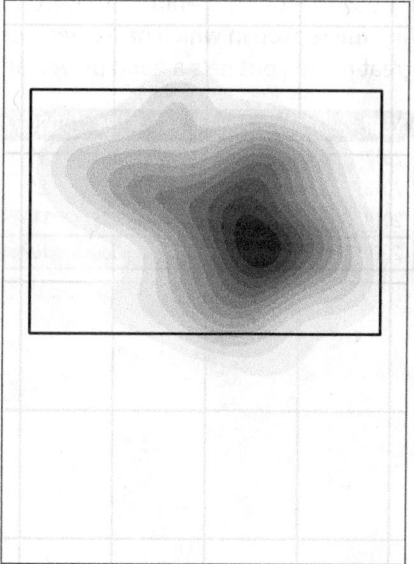

Kole Calhoun RF

Born: 10/14/87   Age: 32   Bats: L   Throws: L
Height: 5'10"   Weight: 215   Origin: Round 8, 2010 Draft (#264 overall)

YEAR	TEAM	LVL	AGE	PA	R	2B	3B	HR	RBI	BB	K	SB	CS	AVG/OBP/SLG
2017	LAA	MLB	29	654	77	23	2	19	71	71	134	5	1	.244/.333/.392
2018	LAA	MLB	30	552	71	18	2	19	57	53	133	6	2	.208/.283/.369
2019	LAA	MLB	31	632	92	29	1	33	74	70	162	4	1	.232/.325/.467
2020	ARI	MLB	32	560	70	23	2	28	80	56	145	4	2	.240/.322/.461

Comparables: Cody Ross, Kevin Kiermaier, Andruw Jones

Nothing typifies the offensively-addled fever dream of the 2019 season than waking up on a random September morning, looking over box scores and player updates, and seeing that Calhoun—Kole Calhoun? really?—has surpassed the 30-home run milestone. In the present era of fast, cheap, and out-of-control offense, it's easy to wave away this benchmark, but it's harder to dismiss the all-around player Calhoun has become. In the three categories that make up WARP for position players—hitting, baserunning, and fielding—Calhoun enjoyed the first full season in which he earned positive marks in all categories. He's not a great player, but he's a good player, and probably better than you think.

YEAR	TEAM	LVL	AGE	PA	DRC+	VORP	BABIP	BRR	FRAA	WARP
2017	LAA	MLB	29	654	99	11.6	.284	-0.6	RF(154): 10.0	2.3
2018	LAA	MLB	30	552	85	-3.3	.241	-0.2		-0.2
2019	LAA	MLB	31	632	110	23.5	.265	0.6		3.1
2020	ARI	MLB	32	560	102	13.1	.283	-0.3	RF 1	1.5

Kole Calhoun, continued

Batted Ball Distribution

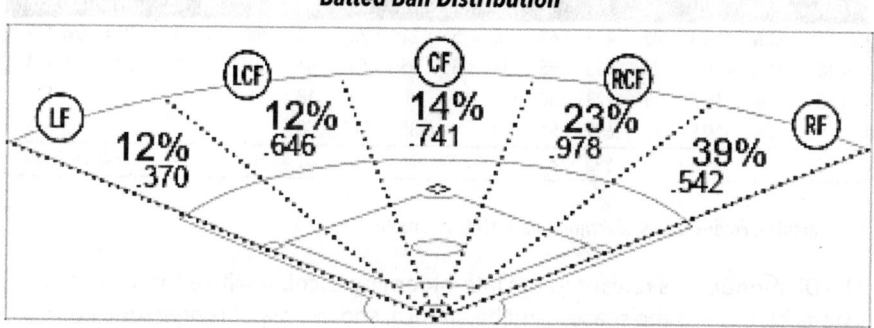

Strike Zone vs LHP   **Strike Zone vs RHP**

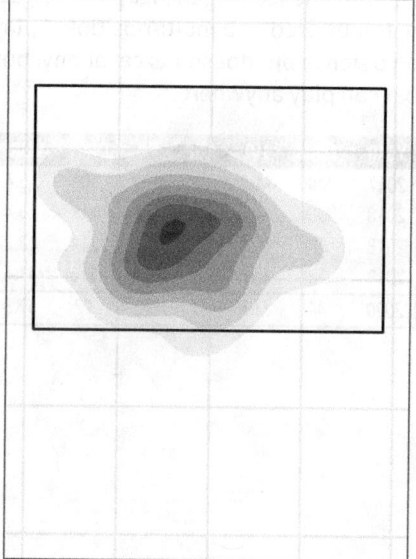

Eduardo Escobar 3B

Born: 01/05/89 Age: 31 Bats: B Throws: R
Height: 5'10" Weight: 185 Origin: International Free Agent, 2006

YEAR	TEAM	LVL	AGE	PA	R	2B	3B	HR	RBI	BB	K	SB	CS	AVG/OBP/SLG
2017	MIN	MLB	28	499	62	16	5	21	73	33	98	5	1	.254/.309/.449
2018	MIN	MLB	29	408	45	37	3	15	63	34	91	1	3	.274/.338/.514
2018	ARI	MLB	29	223	30	11	0	8	21	18	35	1	1	.268/.327/.444
2019	ARI	MLB	30	699	94	29	10	35	118	50	130	5	1	.269/.320/.511
2020	ARI	MLB	31	595	69	27	7	26	83	41	116	4	2	.254/.310/.469

Comparables: Freddy Galvis, Marwin Gonzalez, Alex Gonzalez

The Diamondbacks rewarded the late-blooming Escobar with a three-year extension prior to the season and he, in turn, showed that his breakout was no fluke. Long valued for his defensive utility, Escobar emerged as Arizona's primary third baseman and, while his defense at the hot corner leaves a lot to be desired, he made up for it with the stick by topping his career-high in dingers by a dozen and leading the league in three-baggers. Escobar would likely still be better utilized as a multi-positional player, given that he can handle many spots on defense but doesn't excel at any, but there's no question at this point that his bat can play anywhere.

YEAR	TEAM	LVL	AGE	PA	DRC+	VORP	BABIP	BRR	FRAA	WARP
2017	MIN	MLB	28	499	100	15.4	.279	2.3	3B(79): -5.1, SS(16): -0.5	1.3
2018	MIN	MLB	29	408	115	26.4	.325	-0.1	3B(77): -2.1, SS(21): 0.0	2.1
2018	ARI	MLB	29	223	114	12.3	.281	0.5	3B(54): -4.9	0.8
2019	ARI	MLB	30	699	116	41.4	.283	-0.6	3B(144): -8.4, 2B(33): 1.1	3.3
2020	ARI	MLB	31	595	97	17.8	.280	0.6	2B 2, 3B -3	1.8

Eduardo Escobar, continued

Batted Ball Distribution

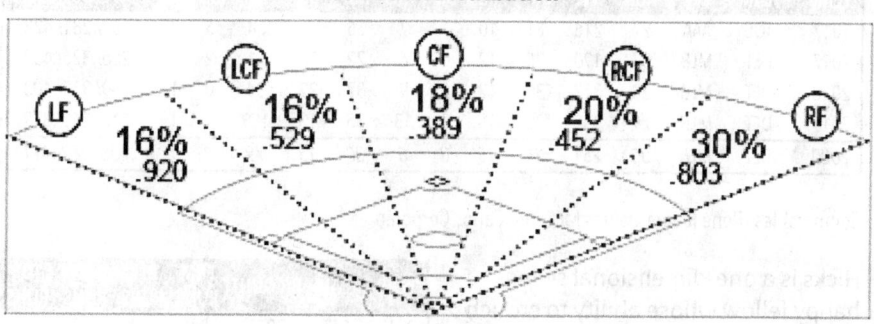

Strike Zone vs LHP   **Strike Zone vs RHP**

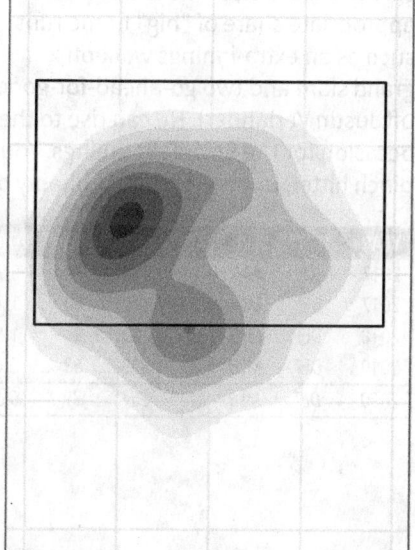

Arizona Diamondbacks 2020

John Hicks C
Born: 08/31/89 Age: 30 Bats: R Throws: R
Height: 6'2" Weight: 230 Origin: Round 4, 2011 Draft (#123 overall)

YEAR	TEAM	LVL	AGE	PA	R	2B	3B	HR	RBI	BB	K	SB	CS	AVG/OBP/SLG
2017	TOL	AAA	27	218	21	10	1	7	35	4	54	5	3	.269/.281/.428
2017	DET	MLB	27	190	25	12	0	6	22	13	51	2	1	.266/.326/.439
2018	DET	MLB	28	312	35	12	1	9	32	22	84	0	1	.260/.312/.403
2019	DET	MLB	29	333	29	15	0	13	35	13	109	1	1	.210/.240/.379
2020	DET	MLB	30	251	25	15	0	8	30	13	79	3	1	.238/.282/.411

Comparables: René Rivera, James McCann, Carlos Corporán

YEAR	TEAM	P. COUNT	FRM RUNS	BLK RUNS	THRW RUNS	TOT RUNS
2017	DET	2077	0.9	-0.1	0.0	1.2
2017	TOL	4951	2.8	0.5	0.0	3.6
2018	DET	2984	-0.9	-0.9	-0.1	-1.9
2019	DET	8575	-7.4	-1.3	0.2	-8.6
2020	DET	4854	-1.5	-0.4	0.1	-1.8

Hicks is a one-dimensional swing-happy fellow whose ability to crouch behind home plate, wear protective padding and flash an array of fingers between his knees will extend his career. He did clout more than his appropriate share of "big" home runs, such as an extra-innings walk-off grand slam and two go-ahead-for-good home runs in ninth innings (one of them off Justin Verlander). He can rise to the occasion though he can't sustain the occasion for the first eight innings. You could do worse with a backup catcher/pinch hitter, but you should probably do better.

YEAR	TEAM	LVL	AGE	PA	DRC+	VORP	BABIP	BRR	FRAA	WARP
2017	TOL	AAA	27	210	84	5.9	.325	-0.5	C(37): 3.4, 1B(11): -0.8	0.5
2017	DET	MLB	27	190	80	1.1	.342	-1.0	1B(26): -0.4, C(18): 0.8	-0.1
2018	DET	MLB	28	312	91	1.6	.337	-1.3	1B(59): 0.3, C(21): -2.3	0.0
2019	DET	MLB	29	333	63	-2.8	.273	-1.6	C(60): -8.1, 1B(29): -1.5	-1.4
2020	DET	MLB	30	251	79	0.6	.321	-0.7	C -2, 1B -1	-0.2

John Hicks, continued

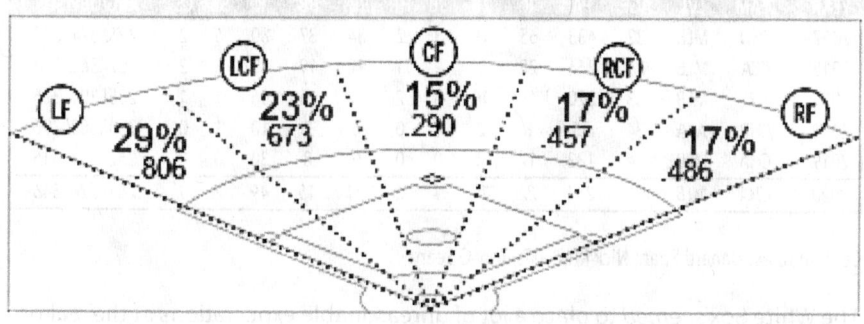

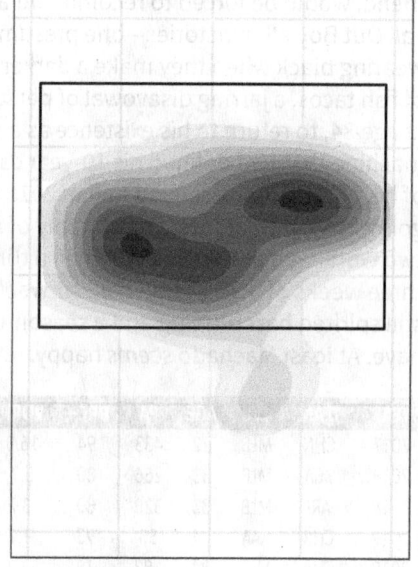

Jon Jay OF

Born: 03/15/85 Age: 35 Bats: L Throws: L
Height: 5'11" Weight: 195 Origin: Round 2, 2006 Draft (#74 overall)

YEAR	TEAM	LVL	AGE	PA	R	2B	3B	HR	RBI	BB	K	SB	CS	AVG/OBP/SLG
2017	CHN	MLB	32	433	65	18	3	2	34	37	80	6	2	.296/.374/.375
2018	KCA	MLB	33	266	28	9	2	1	18	19	39	3	2	.307/.363/.374
2018	ARI	MLB	33	320	46	10	5	2	22	14	56	1	1	.235/.304/.325
2019	CHR	AAA	34	55	8	2	0	0	6	2	10	1	0	.358/.382/.396
2019	CHA	MLB	34	182	12	8	0	0	9	8	30	0	0	.267/.311/.315
2020	CHA	MLB	35	251	22	11	1	2	21	15	49	2	1	.261/.324/.346

Comparables: Denard Span, Nick Markakis, Troy O'Leary

The White Sox *seemed* to place a lot of unreasonable expectations at the feet of Jay when they signed him to a $4 million deal a year ago. As most immediately centered on, they *seemed* to expect him to play a role in recruiting Manny Machado to Chicago. Jay, a respected teammate and Machado's longtime friend, would be forced to recommend a summer at a home stadium that plays Fall Out Boy after victories—one presumes the White Sox won't actually stop wearing black when they make a darker color, but nevertheless—over a decade of fish tacos, a jarring disavowal of personal values. They *seemed* to expect Jay, at age 34, to return to his existence as a slap-hitting/spark-plug on-base machine that had defined his 10-year career, rather than read into the collapse of his offense in the second half of 2018 as a relevant indicator of his capabilities going forward. But, most reasonably of all, they *seemed* to expect him to have two working hips...which, between a three-month absence to start the season, three weeks of pretty good ball, six weeks of pretty awful ball, some very slow if still spirited baserunning and a season-ending surgery, he pretty clearly did not have. At least Machado *seems* happy.

YEAR	TEAM	LVL	AGE	PA	DRC+	VORP	BABIP	BRR	FRAA	WARP
2017	CHN	MLB	32	433	94	16.8	.368	2.4	LF(64): -3.6, CF(54): -4.8	0.2
2018	KCA	MLB	33	266	80	5.9	.360	-0.5	LF(27): 1.2, CF(15): 1.8	0.3
2018	ARI	MLB	33	320	80	-3.7	.284	-0.1	RF(45): 1.9, LF(14): -1.9	-0.1
2019	CHR	AAA	34	55	93	-1.1	.442	0.0	RF(11): -1.4	-0.1
2019	CHA	MLB	34	182	78	-0.9	.324	0.3	RF(33): -4.6, LF(13): -1.6	-0.7
2020	CHA	MLB	35	251	81	2.4	.324	0.4	RF -1, LF -1	-0.1

Jon Jay, continued

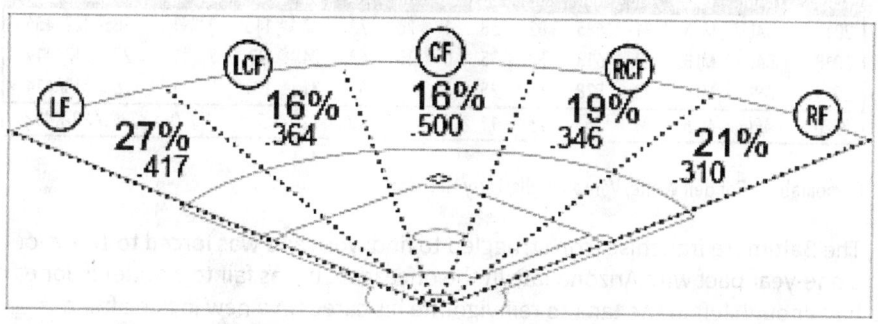

Batted Ball Distribution

| | Strike Zone vs LHP | Strike Zone vs RHP |

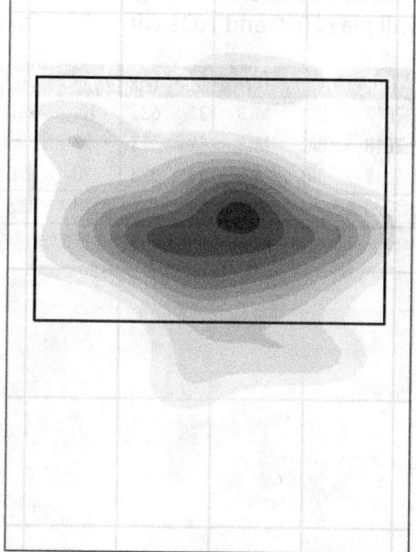

Adam Jones RF

Born: 08/01/85 Age: 34 Bats: R Throws: R
Height: 6'2" Weight: 215 Origin: Round 1, 2003 Draft (#37 overall)

YEAR	TEAM	LVL	AGE	PA	R	2B	3B	HR	RBI	BB	K	SB	CS	AVG/OBP/SLG
2017	BAL	MLB	31	635	82	28	1	26	73	27	113	2	1	.285/.322/.466
2018	BAL	MLB	32	613	54	35	0	15	63	24	93	7	1	.281/.313/.419
2019	ARI	MLB	33	528	66	25	1	16	67	31	101	2	1	.260/.313/.414
2020	ARI	MLB	34	251	26	11	0	8	30	12	51	1	0	.251/.297/.407

Comparables: Rondell White, Vernon Wells, Larry Herndon

The Baltimore franchise icon struggled to find work and was forced to settle for a one-year pact with Arizona late in the offseason. It was fair to wonder if Jones had enough left in the tank to reinvigorate his career in a new locale after a precipitous dip in power and lagging defense forced a move to the corner. The answer was, in a word, no. After a second straight sub-par offensive season, Jones is now firmly in the decline phase of his once-stellar career, and name recognition and his strong locker room reputation will only take him so far. He will play 2020 and 2021 with NPB's Orix Buffaloes.

YEAR	TEAM	LVL	AGE	PA	DRC+	VORP	BABIP	BRR	FRAA	WARP
2017	BAL	MLB	31	635	106	29.2	.312	3.4	CF(147): -4.7	2.6
2018	BAL	MLB	32	613	99	12.4	.311	1.0	CF(106): -11.8, RF(33): 2.0	1.0
2019	ARI	MLB	33	528	90	6.0	.296	1.0	RF(130): -6.2, CF(1): 0.0	0.1
2020	ARI	MLB	34	251	84	3.6	.289	0.6	CF -3, RF 0	0.0

Adam Jones, continued

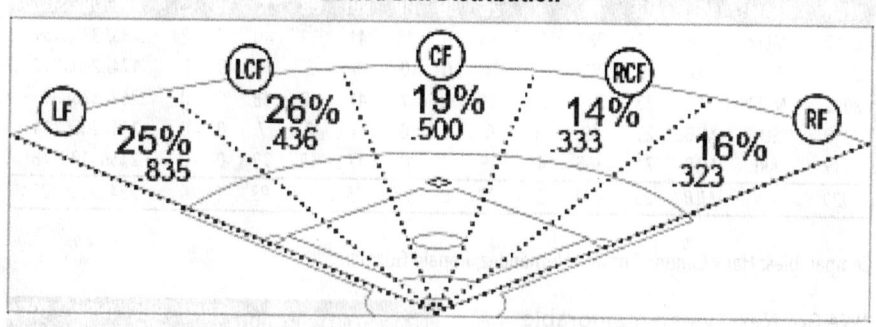

Batted Ball Distribution

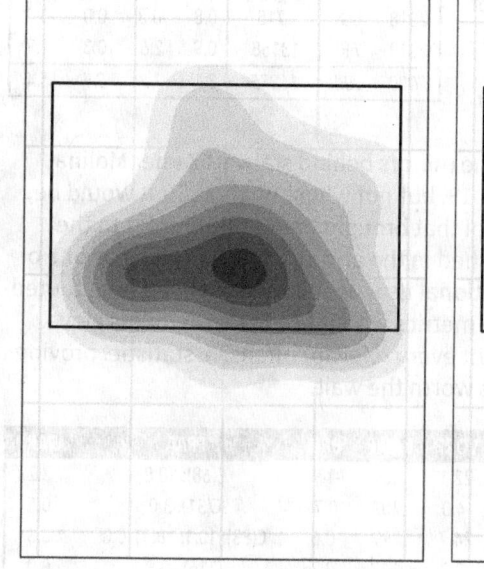

Strike Zone vs LHP

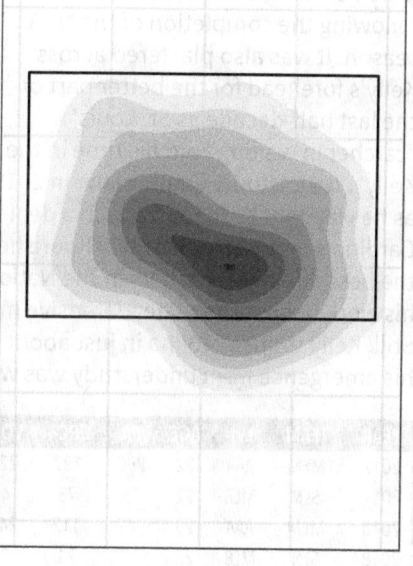

Strike Zone vs RHP

Arizona Diamondbacks 2020

Carson Kelly C
Born: 07/14/94 Age: 25 Bats: R Throws: R
Height: 6'2" Weight: 220 Origin: Round 2, 2012 Draft (#86 overall)

YEAR	TEAM	LVL	AGE	PA	R	2B	3B	HR	RBI	BB	K	SB	CS	AVG/OBP/SLG
2017	MEM	AAA	22	280	37	13	0	10	41	33	40	0	2	.283/.375/.459
2017	SLN	MLB	22	75	5	3	0	0	6	5	11	0	0	.174/.240/.217
2018	MEM	AAA	23	349	38	14	1	7	41	48	48	0	0	.269/.378/.395
2018	SLN	MLB	23	42	1	0	0	0	3	3	7	0	0	.114/.205/.114
2019	ARI	MLB	24	365	46	19	0	18	47	48	79	0	0	.245/.348/.478
2020	ARI	MLB	25	434	50	21	0	17	55	46	93	1	0	.234/.323/.421

Comparables: Hank Conger, Enrique Hernández, Ronald Guzmán

"We Got Next" was a memorable marketing slogan used by the WNBA in the lead-up to the league's inaugural season in 1997, a way to indicate they were next in line for viewers' attention following the completion of the NBA season. It was also plastered across Kelly's forehead for the better part of the last half-decade as St. Louis' "catcher in waiting" bid his time in the minors behind stalwart Yadier Molina. Kelly's opportunity finally came in 2019, but not where he thought it would be, as he was sent to the Arizona in a deal that brought Paul Goldschmidt to the Cardinals. A desert rose, Kelly flourished in the arid climate, emerging as one of the best offensive catchers in the National League. While scouts had long touted his work behind the plate, defensive metrics weren't so in love with his glove. Still, Kelly topped Molina in just about every relevant offensive statistic, proving his emergence from understudy was worth the wait.

YEAR	TEAM	P. COUNT	FRM RUNS	BLK RUNS	THRW RUNS	TOT RUNS
2017	MEM	9388	11.5	1.2	-0.1	12.2
2017	SLN	2565	2.5	0.4	0.1	3.2
2018	MEM	11582	9.0	0.5	0.7	9.9
2018	SLN	1715	-0.8	-0.3	0.0	-1.1
2019	ARI	13168	-0.9	2.6	0.3	1.9
2020	ARI	16275	3.4	1.2	0.9	5.4

YEAR	TEAM	LVL	AGE	PA	DRC+	VORP	BABIP	BRR	FRAA	WARP
2017	MEM	AAA	22	280	127	22.1	.304	-1.9	C(68): 10.8	3.2
2017	SLN	MLB	22	75	73	-4.0	.207	0.7	C(31): 3.0	0.5
2018	MEM	AAA	23	349	112	24.7	.299	-0.6	C(83): 10.1, 1B(1): 0.0	3.3
2018	SLN	MLB	23	42	74	-3.2	.143	-0.2	C(16): -0.9	0.0
2019	ARI	MLB	24	365	115	26.4	.271	-1.2	C(101): -0.1, 3B(1): 0.0	2.5
2020	ARI	MLB	25	434	101	20.8	.267	-0.3	C 4	2.6

Carson Kelly, continued

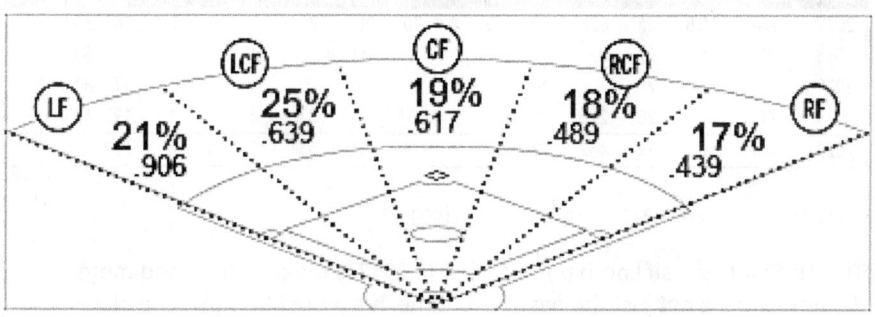

Batted Ball Distribution

Strike Zone vs LHP **Strike Zone vs RHP**

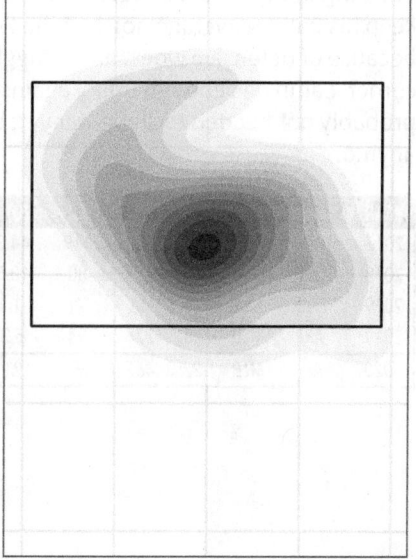

Arizona Diamondbacks 2020

Jake Lamb CI
Born: 10/09/90 Age: 29 Bats: L Throws: R
Height: 6'3" Weight: 215 Origin: Round 6, 2012 Draft (#213 overall)

YEAR	TEAM	LVL	AGE	PA	R	2B	3B	HR	RBI	BB	K	SB	CS	AVG/OBP/SLG
2017	ARI	MLB	26	635	89	30	4	30	105	87	152	6	4	.248/.357/.487
2018	ARI	MLB	27	238	34	8	0	6	31	26	65	1	2	.222/.307/.348
2019	RNO	AAA	28	46	5	2	0	1	7	7	12	0	0	.179/.304/.308
2019	ARI	MLB	28	226	26	8	2	6	30	32	55	1	0	.193/.323/.353
2020	ARI	MLB	29	462	53	20	4	16	57	55	127	4	2	.227/.326/.420

Comparables: Shane Andrews, Pedro Álvarez, Evan Longoria

The All-Star first half Lamb put together in 2017 is looking more and more distant, and it's not just the passage of time. It's more likely that the player Lamb is going to be is the player he's been the last two seasons: an injury-prone platoon bat. Lamb has fewer than 500 plate appearances to his name the last two seasons combined, as a shoulder injury ended his 2018 season early and a quad injury derailed his 2019. During the rare healthy times, he's struggled to keep his batting average north of the Mendoza line, was moved off of third base because of defensive woes, and struggled to adjust to his new home at the cold corner. Lamb has enough utility against right-handed pitchers that he's probably not headed to slaughter yet, but that fleece isn't exactly white as snow anymore.

YEAR	TEAM	LVL	AGE	PA	DRC+	VORP	BABIP	BRR	FRAA	WARP
2017	ARI	MLB	26	635	119	44.2	.287	2.0	3B(144): -10.8	2.9
2018	ARI	MLB	27	238	80	10.5	.286	1.6	3B(52): -3.7	0.0
2019	RNO	AAA	28	46	71	-1.4	.231	0.0	3B(6): -0.8, 1B(5): 0.0	-0.1
2019	ARI	MLB	28	226	94	5.2	.234	2.3	3B(36): -1.6, 1B(24): -1.3	0.4
2020	ARI	MLB	29	462	93	9.9	.290	2.3	3B -6, 1B -1	0.3

Jake Lamb, continued

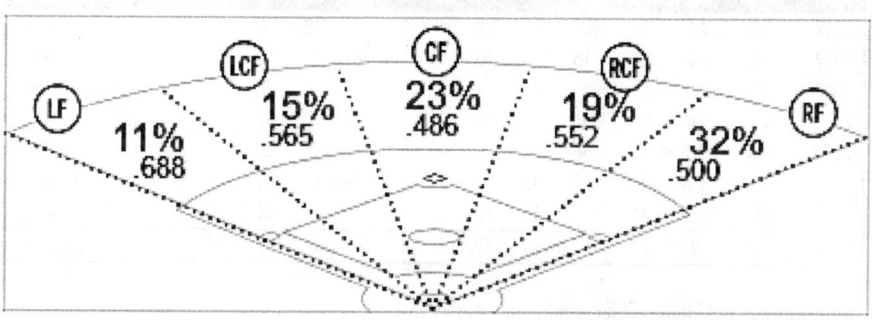

Batted Ball Distribution

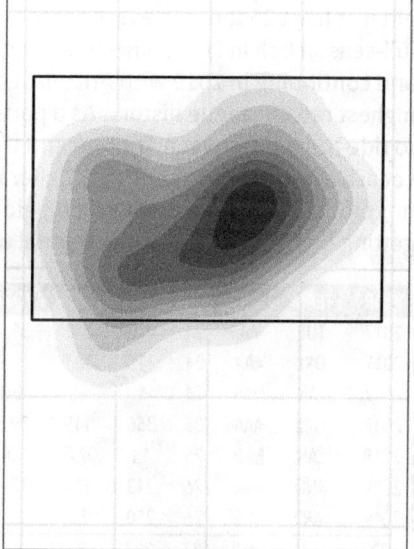

Strike Zone vs LHP   **Strike Zone vs RHP**

Arizona Diamondbacks 2020

Tim Locastro OF
Born: 07/14/92 Age: 27 Bats: R Throws: R
Height: 6'1" Weight: 200 Origin: Round 13, 2013 Draft (#385 overall)

YEAR	TEAM	LVL	AGE	PA	R	2B	3B	HR	RBI	BB	K	SB	CS	AVG/OBP/SLG
2017	TUL	AA	24	420	69	21	4	8	31	22	56	22	5	.285/.366/.429
2017	OKL	AAA	24	115	18	10	0	2	9	6	12	12	2	.388/.443/.544
2017	LAN	MLB	24	1	0	0	0	0	0	0	0	1	0	.000/.000/.000
2018	OKL	AAA	25	356	61	23	2	4	25	28	52	18	2	.279/.389/.409
2018	LAN	MLB	25	14	6	1	0	0	0	2	5	4	0	.182/.357/.273
2019	RNO	AAA	26	143	35	11	2	8	21	10	24	9	1	.301/.394/.618
2019	ARI	MLB	26	250	38	12	2	1	17	14	44	17	0	.250/.357/.340
2020	ARI	MLB	27	287	30	12	1	6	29	16	52	12	3	.236/.329/.367

Comparables: Cord Phelps, Cliff Pennington, Scott Sizemore

On May 24, Locastro came to bat six times in the Diamondbacks' 18-2 win over the Giants. He reached base four of those times in the blowout, with three free passes via the HBP. This was nothing new for Locastro, who has been hit by a pitch at least 25 times in every season (majors and minors) since his first year in full-season ball in 2014. Since reaching the majors, first with cups of coffee in LA and continuing in 2019 with Arizona, Locastro's HBP rate is 8.7 percent, the highest rate in league history. As a part-time outfielder who will likely continue to ride the bus between Triple-A and the big leagues whenever a need arises, Locastro is unlikely to sniff deadballer Hughie Jennings' career record of 287, nor modern day specialist Craig Biggio's 285, but he clearly has a knack for getting on base in an unconventional way.

YEAR	TEAM	LVL	AGE	PA	DRC+	VORP	BABIP	BRR	FRAA	WARP
2017	TUL	AA	24	420	131	31.2	.317	5.4	CF(46): -2.3, SS(31): -3.9	2.5
2017	OKL	AAA	24	115	161	15.9	.422	1.7	2B(22): -2.0, LF(8): 0.0	1.2
2017	LAN	MLB	24	1	95	-0.3	.000	0.0	LF(2): -0.1	0.0
2018	OKL	AAA	25	356	119	29.2	.327	4.2	CF(46): -3.7, 2B(30): -1.8	2.0
2018	LAN	MLB	25	14	77	1.4	.333	0.4	CF(4): -0.1, LF(1): 0.0	0.0
2019	RNO	AAA	26	143	117	12.8	.319	1.9	CF(20): -1.4, RF(7): -0.2	0.7
2019	ARI	MLB	26	250	85	2.6	.310	0.3	LF(34): 1.6, RF(25): 0.0	0.2
2020	ARI	MLB	27	287	93	6.3	.275	-1.0	CF -4, LF 1	0.4

Tim Locastro, continued

Batted Ball Distribution

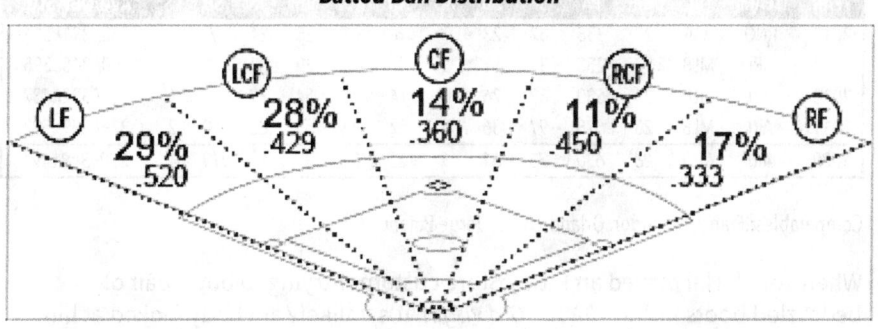

Strike Zone vs LHP

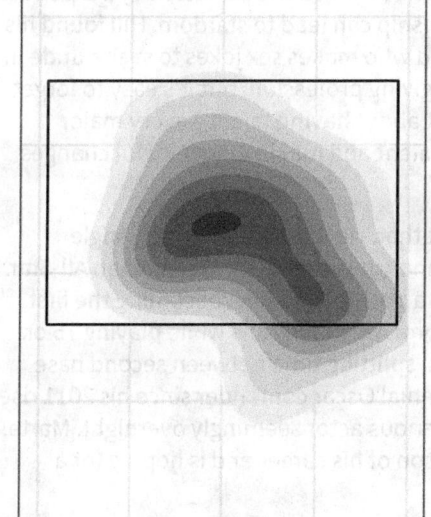

Strike Zone vs RHP

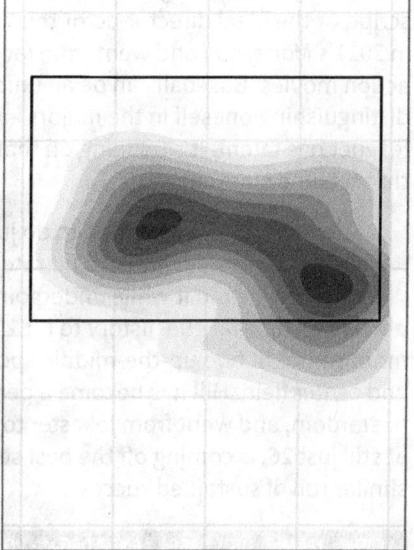

Arizona Diamondbacks 2020

Ketel Marte CF
Born: 10/12/93 Age: 26 Bats: B Throws: R
Height: 6'1" Weight: 165 Origin: International Free Agent, 2010

YEAR	TEAM	LVL	AGE	PA	R	2B	3B	HR	RBI	BB	K	SB	CS	AVG/OBP/SLG
2017	RNO	AAA	23	338	62	23	7	6	41	25	34	7	2	.338/.391/.514
2017	ARI	MLB	23	255	30	11	2	5	18	29	37	3	1	.260/.345/.395
2018	ARI	MLB	24	580	68	26	12	14	59	54	79	6	1	.260/.332/.437
2019	ARI	MLB	25	628	97	36	9	32	92	53	86	10	2	.329/.389/.592
2020	ARI	MLB	26	630	75	31	9	22	84	49	93	13	4	.290/.348/.491

Comparables: Francisco Lindor, Orlando Arcia, Jorge Polanco

When Jonah Hill played an E-Bay Store customer trying to buy a pair of bedazzled boots in *The 40-Year-Old Virgin*, it's unlikely anybody looked at him and said "that guy's going to be an Academy Award nominee one day." Similarly, when Marte was a light-hitting middle infielder for the Mariners, it's unlikely anybody looked at him and said "that guy's going to be an All-Star one day." Acting is an unforgiving profession, but one in which the perfect role, the perfect script, or the ideal director-actor relationship can lead to stardom. Hill found his in 2011's *Moneyball* and went from fat kid who makes sex jokes to svelte dude in action movies. Baseball can be an unforgiving profession, but it's easy to forget distinguishing oneself in the majors isn't about having talent—every major leaguer has talent. It's building on that talent and making meaningful changes that sets the stars apart.

Marte found the right recipe to do just that. He joined the Launch Angle Revolution, increased his hard hit rate, and transformed himself into an All-Star. What's more, he did it while undergoing a position change, becoming the first player in major-league history to hit 25 or more home runs while playing 75 or more games at two up-the-middle spots, splitting time between second base and center field. Hill has become a perennial Oscar contender since his 2011 rise to stardom, and went from jokester to serious actor seemingly overnight. Marte, at still just 26, is coming off the best season of his career and is hoping for a similar run of sustained success.

YEAR	TEAM	LVL	AGE	PA	DRC+	VORP	BABIP	BRR	FRAA	WARP
2017	RNO	AAA	23	338	124	31.9	.365	3.8	SS(59): 2.1, CF(5): 1.6	3.3
2017	ARI	MLB	23	255	100	13.9	.290	1.5	SS(64): -0.1, 3B(3): 0.1	1.3
2018	ARI	MLB	24	580	102	28.0	.282	0.6	2B(131): 4.5, SS(28): 1.8	2.9
2019	ARI	MLB	25	628	141	56.4	.342	1.9	CF(96): -8.3, 2B(83): -2.9	4.5
2020	ARI	MLB	26	630	114	36.2	.313	1.0	CF -6, 2B 0	3.2

Ketel Marte, continued

Batted Ball Distribution

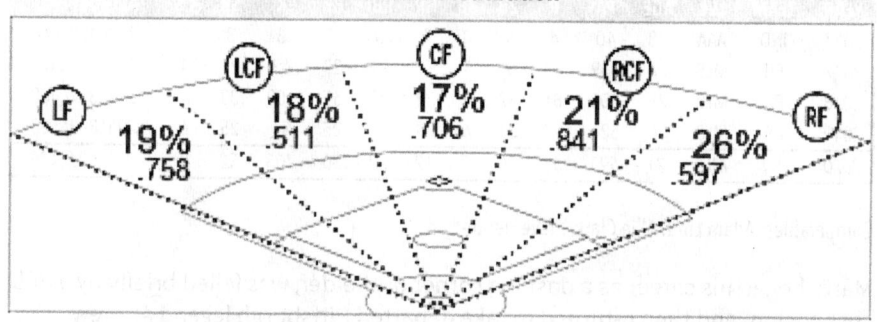

Strike Zone vs LHP   **Strike Zone vs RHP**

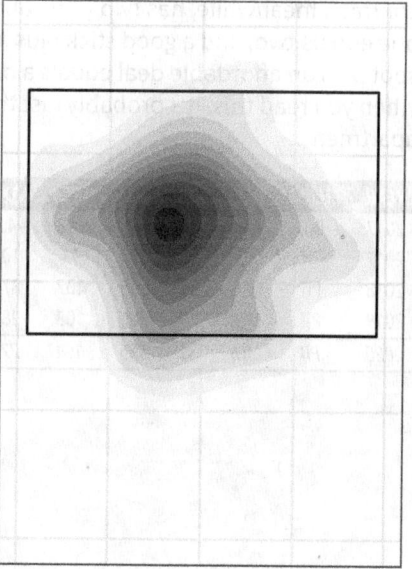

Arizona Diamondbacks 2020

Starling Marte CF
Born: 10/09/88 Age: 31 Bats: R Throws: R
Height: 6'1" Weight: 190 Origin: International Free Agent, 2007

YEAR	TEAM	LVL	AGE	PA	R	2B	3B	HR	RBI	BB	K	SB	CS	AVG/OBP/SLG
2017	IND	AAA	28	40	4	1	0	1	3	2	8	3	0	.333/.400/.444
2017	PIT	MLB	28	339	48	7	2	7	31	20	63	21	4	.275/.333/.379
2018	PIT	MLB	29	606	81	32	5	20	72	35	109	33	14	.277/.327/.460
2019	PIT	MLB	30	586	97	31	6	23	82	25	94	25	6	.295/.342/.503
2020	PIT	MLB	31	595	68	30	3	19	72	30	108	32	10	.270/.326/.439

Comparables: Adam Lind, Allie Clark, Steve Henderson

Marte began his career as a dashing corner outfielder, was felled briefly by a PED suspension, and then returned to take departed Pittsburgh legend Andrew McCutchen's place in center. He's now reached the final and truest stage of development one can achieve as a Pirate: trade chit. The remade Pirates front office is likely to reimagine the roster sooner than later. Marte's team-friendly contract, meanwhile, has two years and $24 million remaining on it. One plus one equals two, and a good stick plus an established glove in a corner-outfield spot plus an affordable deal equals a marketable asset. If he's in Pittsburgh when you read this, it's probably just to visit some friends or to pack up his apartment.

YEAR	TEAM	LVL	AGE	PA	DRC+	VORP	BABIP	BRR	FRAA	WARP
2017	IND	AAA	28	40	118	4.6	.407	0.9	LF(6): -0.4, CF(1): 0.1	0.2
2017	PIT	MLB	28	339	91	10.2	.324	3.4	LF(56): 5.9, CF(25): 3.1	1.8
2018	PIT	MLB	29	606	107	37.2	.312	0.1	CF(139): 7.0	3.4
2019	PIT	MLB	30	586	108	28.1	.319	3.9	CF(130): 2.3	3.4
2020	PIT	MLB	31	595	104	27.2	.306	1.9	CF 4	3.2

Starling Marte, continued

Batted Ball Distribution

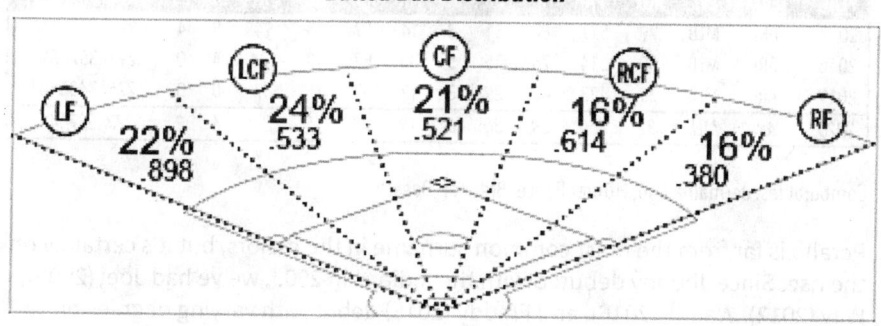

Strike Zone vs LHP **Strike Zone vs RHP**

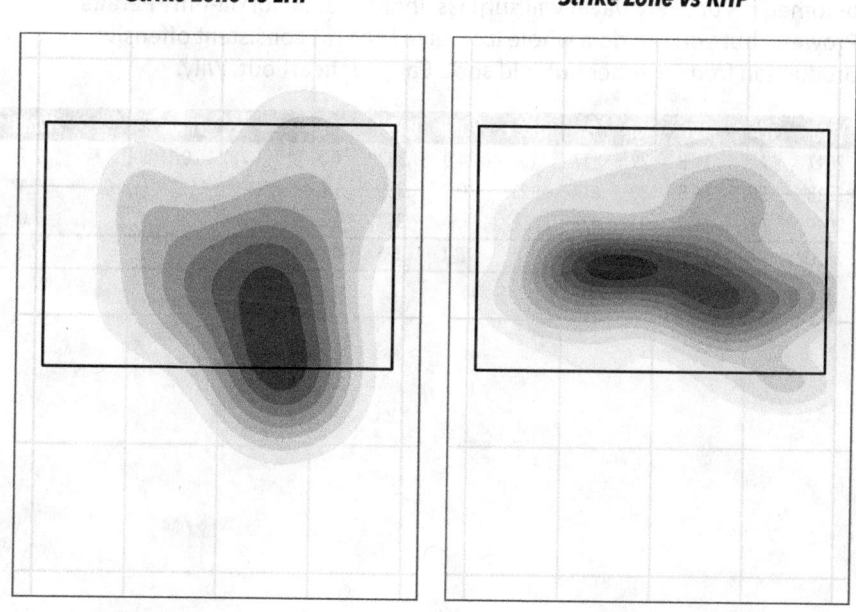

Diamondbacks Player Analysis - 41

Arizona Diamondbacks 2020

David Peralta LF
Born: 08/14/87   Age: 32   Bats: L   Throws: L
Height: 6'1"   Weight: 210   Origin: International Free Agent, 2005

YEAR	TEAM	LVL	AGE	PA	R	2B	3B	HR	RBI	BB	K	SB	CS	AVG/OBP/SLG
2017	ARI	MLB	29	577	82	31	3	14	57	43	94	8	4	.293/.352/.444
2018	ARI	MLB	30	614	75	25	5	30	87	48	124	4	0	.293/.352/.516
2019	ARI	MLB	31	423	48	29	3	12	57	35	87	0	0	.275/.343/.461
2020	ARI	MLB	32	560	64	30	6	19	72	45	120	6	2	.273/.337/.467

Comparables: Jermaine Dye, Hunter Pence, Brennan Boesch

Peralta is far from the most common surname in the majors, but it's certainly on the rise. Since Jhonny debuted with the Indians in 2003, we've had Joel (2005), Wily (2012), Wandy (2016), and Freddy (2018) debut with varying degrees of notoriety. David (10.3) passed Joel (8.6) for second place on the all-time Peralta WARP leaderboard, despite missing a third of the campaign with injury. A late bloomer, it's unlikely David will surpass Jhonny (31.8) for all-time Peralta Prowess, but you can do a whole lot worse than his consistent offensive production from a corner outfield spot. Eat your heart out, Wily.

YEAR	TEAM	LVL	AGE	PA	DRC+	VORP	BABIP	BRR	FRAA	WARP
2017	ARI	MLB	29	577	103	24.0	.333	-0.9	RF(78): 10.0, LF(50): 2.2	2.7
2018	ARI	MLB	30	614	121	40.7	.328	1.2	LF(138): -11.0, RF(5): -0.5	2.1
2019	ARI	MLB	31	423	97	9.9	.327	-2.8	LF(93): 13.4	2.0
2020	ARI	MLB	32	560	105	18.1	.325	-0.9	LF 3	2.2

David Peralta, continued

Batted Ball Distribution

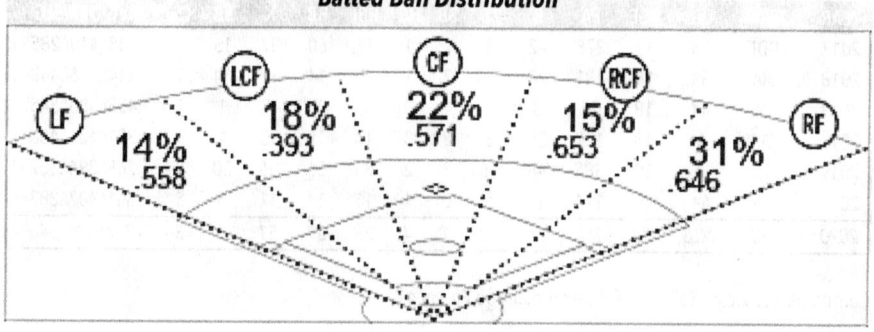

Strike Zone vs LHP **Strike Zone vs RHP**

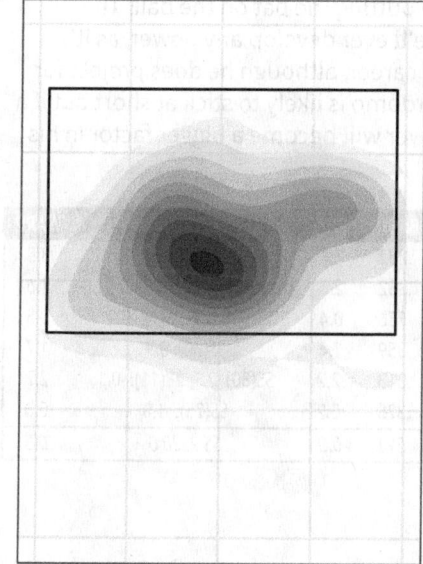 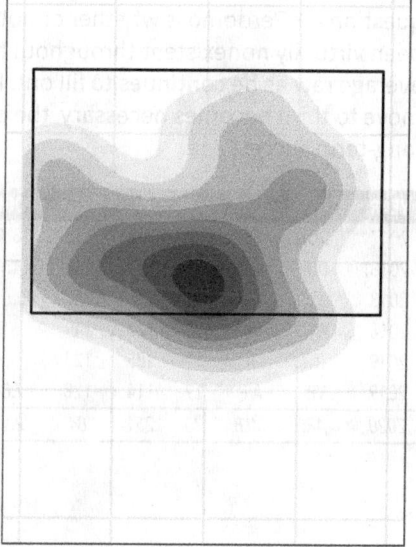

Arizona Diamondbacks 2020

Geraldo Perdomo SS
Born: 10/22/99   Age: 20   Bats: B   Throws: R
Height: 6'3"   Weight: 184   Origin: International Free Agent, 2016

YEAR	TEAM	LVL	AGE	PA	R	2B	3B	HR	RBI	BB	K	SB	CS	AVG/OBP/SLG
2017	DDI	RK	17	278	42	3	2	1	11	60	37	16	8	.238/.410/.285
2018	DIA	RK	18	101	20	4	2	1	8	14	17	14	1	.314/.416/.442
2018	MSO	RK	18	29	3	0	1	0	2	7	4	1	1	.455/.586/.545
2018	YAK	A-	18	127	20	3	2	3	14	18	23	9	4	.301/.421/.456
2019	KNC	A	19	385	48	16	3	2	36	56	56	20	8	.268/.394/.357
2019	VIS	A+	19	114	15	5	0	1	11	14	11	6	5	.301/.407/.387
2020	ARI	MLB	20	251	25	10	1	4	23	27	51	6	3	.237/.329/.346

Comparables: Victor Robles, J.P. Crawford, Jorge Polanco

Perdomo is somewhat unique for an up-the-middle prospect, especially one with his youth and skills. Namely, he already has a solid grasp of the strike zone and there's little swing-and-miss in his game. Across two levels, he walked more than he struck out and never had an issue putting the bat on the ball. The question for Perdomo is whether or not he'll ever develop any power, as it's been virtually nonexistent throughout his career, although he does project for average raw as he continues to fill out. Perdomo is likely to stick at short but if a move to third becomes necessary, the power will become a bigger factor in his long-term success.

YEAR	TEAM	LVL	AGE	PA	DRC+	VORP	BABIP	BRR	FRAA	WARP
2017	DDI	RK	17	278	135	18.4	.282	1.4	SS(63): 11.9	3.5
2018	DIA	RK	18	101	168	14.9	.382	2.6	SS(14): 2.6, 2B(8): 0.5	1.6
2018	MSO	RK	18	29	248	6.6	.556	0.4	SS(5): 0.3, 2B(1): -0.2	0.5
2018	YAK	A-	18	127	149	16.1	.359	1.4	SS(30): 3.9	1.7
2019	KNC	A	19	385	127	25.7	.318	-2.2	SS(80): 2.1, 2B(11): -0.1	2.7
2019	VIS	A+	19	114	128	7.8	.325	-0.2	SS(25): -1.0	0.6
2020	ARI	MLB	20	251	84	2.9	.291	0.0	SS 2, 2B 0	0.5

Geraldo Perdomo, continued

Batted Ball Distribution

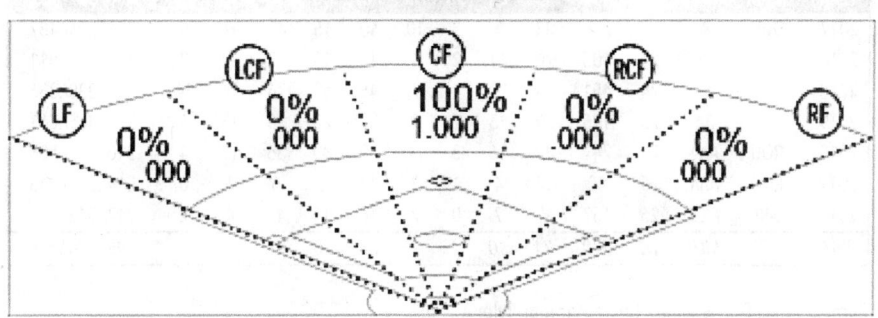

Strike Zone vs LHP **Strike Zone vs RHP**

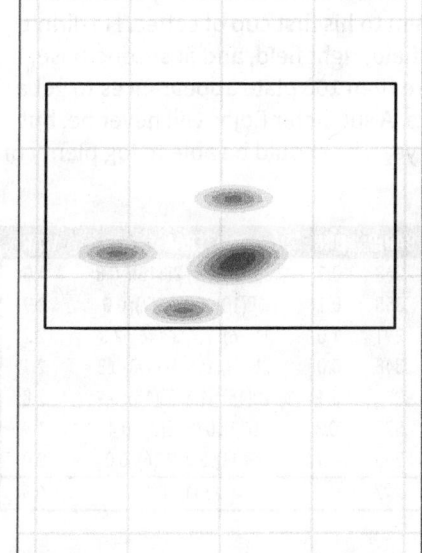
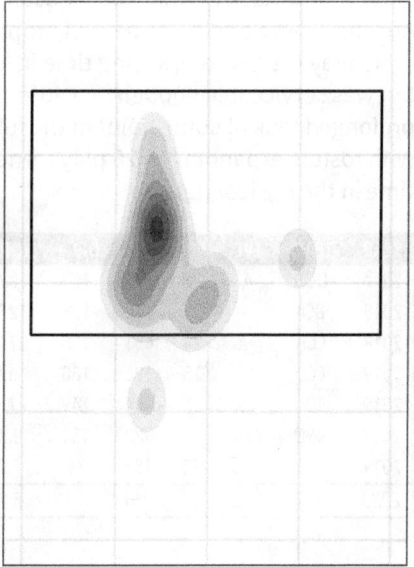

Arizona Diamondbacks 2020

Josh Rojas UT
Born: 06/30/94   Age: 26   Bats: L   Throws: R
Height: 6'1"   Weight: 185   Origin: Round 26, 2017 Draft (#781 overall)

YEAR	TEAM	LVL	AGE	PA	R	2B	3B	HR	RBI	BB	K	SB	CS	AVG/OBP/SLG
2017	QUD	A	23	219	33	5	5	10	40	15	43	0	0	.256/.306/.487
2018	BCA	A+	24	105	20	11	2	1	10	15	13	12	0	.311/.410/.511
2018	CCH	AA	24	451	64	23	4	7	45	53	76	26	14	.251/.338/.385
2019	CCH	AA	25	195	29	13	2	8	30	22	28	13	6	.322/.405/.561
2019	ROU	AAA	25	244	49	16	3	12	39	30	36	19	4	.310/.402/.586
2019	RNO	AAA	25	40	11	4	1	3	14	5	6	1	0	.514/.575/.943
2019	ARI	MLB	25	157	17	7	0	2	16	18	41	4	2	.217/.312/.312
2020	ARI	MLB	26	210	24	10	2	7	26	20	48	7	3	.249/.326/.438

Comparables: Bob Nieman, Mitch Haniger, Tyler Austin

A player of Rojas' ilk has plenty of utility in today's game, given his ability to adequately handle every infield position and the corners in the outfield. His move, in the Zack Greinke blockbuster, from Houston's loaded organization to Arizona's more arid clime helped propel him to his first cup of coffee. He didn't quite play *every*where, seeing time in left field, right field, and at second base, but was serviceable enough in a little more than 100 plate appearances to get a prolonged look at some point in the future. A superstar Rojas will never be, but with rosters expanding to 26 players next year, he should be able to log plenty of time in the big leagues.

YEAR	TEAM	LVL	AGE	PA	DRC+	VORP	BABIP	BRR	FRAA	WARP
2017	QUD	A	23	219	106	13.6	.268	0.1	3B(30): 0.7, 2B(18): -0.8	1.0
2018	BCA	A+	24	105	158	12.9	.355	0.1	2B(10): 1.0, 1B(7): 0.0	0.9
2018	CCH	AA	24	451	108	17.4	.291	1.0	LF(36): 2.2, 3B(16): 2.3	2.2
2019	CCH	AA	25	195	180	16.6	.348	0.0	2B(30): 0.6, 1B(12): 0.8	2.1
2019	ROU	AAA	25	244	149	27.1	.325	2.1	2B(15): -1.5, SS(15): 0.9	2.8
2019	RNO	AAA	25	40	153	8.3	.577	-0.3	LF(2): 0.0, SS(2): -0.4	1.9
2019	ARI	MLB	25	157	76	-0.7	.295	-1.7	LF(33): 2.7, RF(6): 0.0	0.0
2020	ARI	MLB	26	210	98	5.5	.297	0.6	RF -1, LF 0	0.5

Josh Rojas, continued

Batted Ball Distribution

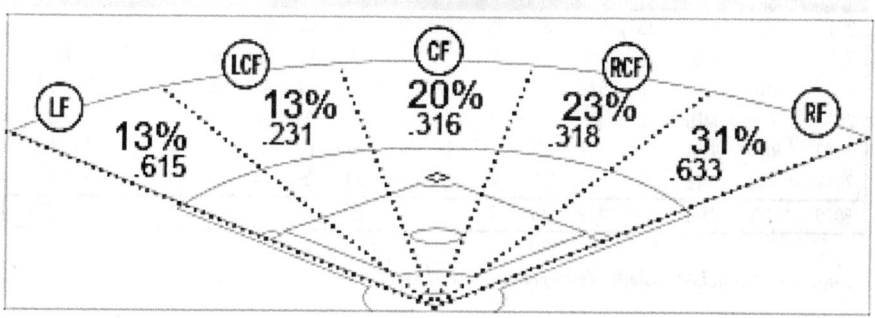

Strike Zone vs LHP   **Strike Zone vs RHP**

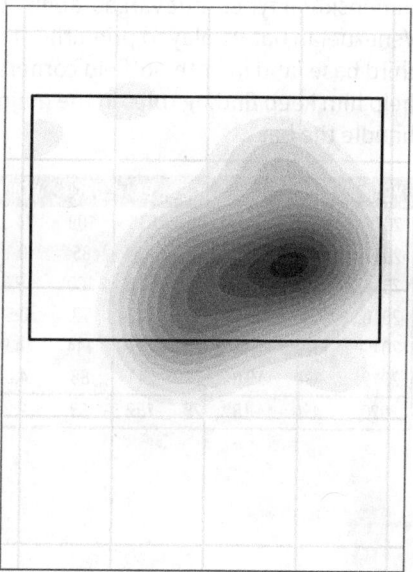

Arizona Diamondbacks 2020

Ildemaro Vargas 2B
Born: 07/16/91 Age: 28 Bats: B Throws: R
Height: 6'0" Weight: 170 Origin: International Free Agent, 2008

YEAR	TEAM	LVL	AGE	PA	R	2B	3B	HR	RBI	BB	K	SB	CS	AVG/OBP/SLG
2017	RNO	AAA	25	535	87	35	4	10	65	30	40	8	3	.312/.355/.462
2017	ARI	MLB	25	13	4	1	0	0	4	0	3	0	0	.308/.308/.385
2018	RNO	AAA	26	572	78	31	10	7	54	30	46	10	4	.311/.348/.445
2018	ARI	MLB	26	20	2	0	0	1	4	1	4	1	0	.211/.250/.368
2019	RNO	AAA	27	137	20	9	3	2	24	11	5	1	1	.403/.453/.573
2019	ARI	MLB	27	211	25	9	1	6	24	9	24	1	0	.269/.299/.413
2020	ARI	MLB	28	189	18	8	1	4	20	10	23	2	1	.268/.311/.394

Comparables: Yangervis Solarte, Kevin Frandsen, Tony Kemp

A car needs oil, a painter needs paint, Kate Winslet needs an American-accented Oscar-bait role, and a major-league roster in 2020 needs a player like Vargas. An additional roster spot this season could create room for the more one-dimensional types, but Vargas' ability to play all over will serve him well. The Venezuelan native played primarily at second base, but saw time at shortstop, third base, and in both outfield corners in 2019, and that kind of utility should help him keep finding roles in the majors going forward. Now, if he could just handle the bat...

YEAR	TEAM	LVL	AGE	PA	DRC+	VORP	BABIP	BRR	FRAA	WARP
2017	RNO	AAA	25	535	108	34.5	.319	1.3	2B(93): 11.8, SS(8): -1.6	3.2
2017	ARI	MLB	25	13	85	-0.1	.400	0.1	2B(3): 0.0, 3B(2): -0.1	0.0
2018	RNO	AAA	26	572	100	19.8	.329	-3.8	SS(107): -6.0, 2B(17): -0.1	1.5
2018	ARI	MLB	26	20	93	0.5	.214	0.0	3B(3): 0.3, 2B(2): 0.1	0.1
2019	RNO	AAA	27	137	144	14.9	.407	1.9	SS(13): 0.8, 3B(12): 0.3	1.6
2019	ARI	MLB	27	211	88	4.0	.279	0.4	2B(48): 2.4, 3B(14): -1.1	0.6
2020	ARI	MLB	28	189	83	2.9	.289	0.1	2B 2, SS 0	0.5

Ildemaro Vargas, continued

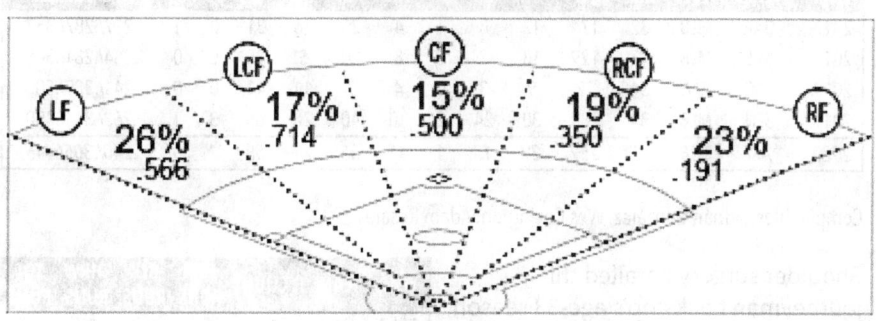

Batted Ball Distribution

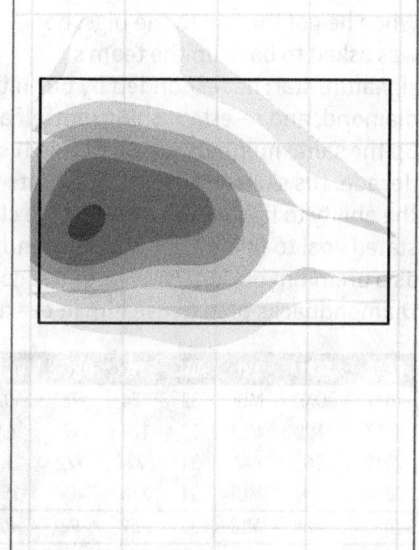

Strike Zone vs LHP

Strike Zone vs RHP

Stephen Vogt   C

Born: 11/01/84   Age: 35   Bats: L   Throws: R
Height: 6'0"   Weight: 225   Origin: Round 12, 2007 Draft (#365 overall)

YEAR	TEAM	LVL	AGE	PA	R	2B	3B	HR	RBI	BB	K	SB	CS	AVG/OBP/SLG
2017	OAK	MLB	32	174	12	8	1	4	20	16	31	0	1	.217/.287/.357
2017	MIL	MLB	32	129	13	7	0	8	20	5	25	0	0	.254/.281/.508
2019	SAC	AAA	34	72	9	3	0	4	7	14	11	0	0	.241/.389/.500
2019	SFN	MLB	34	280	30	24	2	10	40	20	66	3	1	.263/.314/.490
2020	ARI	MLB	35	259	29	13	1	11	35	21	58	1	0	.240/.305/.446

Comparables: Adrián González, Wes Covington, Adam Rosales

YEAR	TEAM	P. COUNT	FRM RUNS	BLK RUNS	THRW RUNS	TOT RUNS
2017	OAK	5443	5.3	0.2	-1.6	3.8
2017	MIL	4322	4.3	1.4	-2.4	3.3
2019	SAC	1361	-0.2	-0.1	-0.2	-0.7
2019	SFN	7684	-1.6	-0.6	-0.5	-3.7
2020	ARI	14501	-4.4	-0.6	-1.6	-6.6

Shoulder surgery derailed this journeyman backstop's age-33 season, so a minor-league contract brought him back to the part of the country where he'd once found success, if not precisely within the same city limits. When he got the call to the bigs, he was asked to back up the team's signature star; he responded by out-hitting Buster Posey, filling in around the diamond, and re-establishing himself as a quality backup, despite not putting up the same numbers he did during his two All-Star seasons in the middle of the decade. His skillset includes moderate power, mediocre defense, versatility, and the ability to lighten the mood in the clubhouse, which dovetails nicely with his stated goal to find a team that contends for the World Series in 2020. Best cast as a premium backup catcher or a second-division starter, the Arizona Diamondbacks plan to use him in exactly that role next year.

YEAR	TEAM	LVL	AGE	PA	DRC+	VORP	BABIP	BRR	FRAA	WARP
2017	OAK	MLB	32	174	92	-0.3	.244	-1.7	C(43): -0.9, LF(1): -0.1	0.3
2017	MIL	MLB	32	129	92	6.9	.256	-1.8	C(38): 0.0	0.3
2019	SAC	AAA	34	72	122	3.1	.233	-0.7	C(9): -0.3, 1B(6): -0.4	0.3
2019	SFN	MLB	34	280	106	15.5	.311	-0.2	C(60): -1.0, LF(7): -0.2	1.4
2020	ARI	MLB	35	259	92	8.5	.273	-1.0	C -6	0.2

Stephen Vogt, continued

Batted Ball Distribution

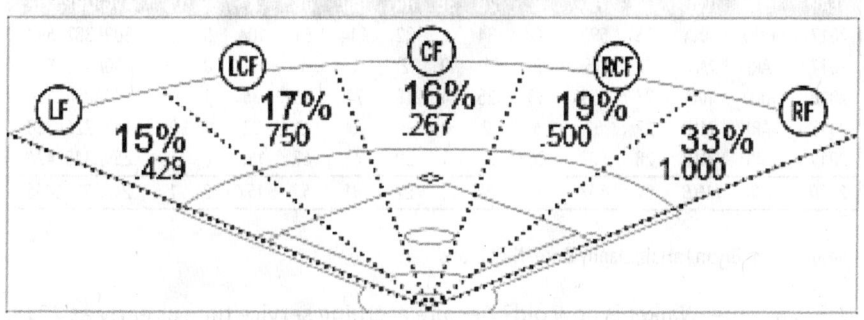

Strike Zone vs LHP   **Strike Zone vs RHP**

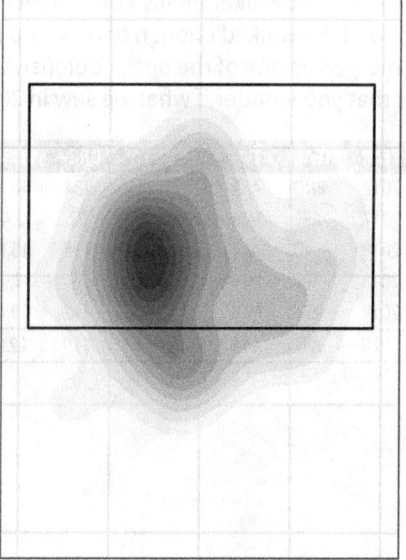

Arizona Diamondbacks 2020

Christian Walker 1B

Born: 03/28/91   Age: 29   Bats: R   Throws: R
Height: 6'0"   Weight: 220   Origin: Round 4, 2012 Draft (#132 overall)

YEAR	TEAM	LVL	AGE	PA	R	2B	3B	HR	RBI	BB	K	SB	CS	AVG/OBP/SLG
2017	RNO	AAA	26	592	104	34	9	32	114	61	104	5	2	.309/.382/.597
2017	ARI	MLB	26	15	2	1	0	2	2	1	5	0	0	.250/.400/.833
2018	RNO	AAA	27	359	68	25	4	18	71	26	86	1	0	.299/.354/.568
2018	ARI	MLB	27	53	6	2	0	3	6	3	22	1	0	.163/.226/.388
2019	ARI	MLB	28	603	86	26	1	29	73	67	155	8	1	.259/.348/.476
2020	ARI	MLB	29	567	70	27	2	27	81	53	157	2	1	.247/.326/.466

Comparables: Bryan LaHair, Danny Dorn, Nick Evans

Wait a minute, Walker is how old? Despite accruing service time as early as 2013, Walker entered 2019 with just 99 career plate appearances, serving instead as minor-league depth over the past five seasons, first behind Chris Davis in Baltimore and then Paul Goldschmidt in Arizona. Thus, it wasn't until his age-28 season that Walker finally got a chance to see regular playing time. The power played, he walked enough to make up for hefty strikeout numbers, and he emerged as one of the better defensive first basemen in the game. The problem is that you wonder if what we saw in 2019 is his ceiling.

YEAR	TEAM	LVL	AGE	PA	DRC+	VORP	BABIP	BRR	FRAA	WARP
2017	RNO	AAA	26	592	134	40.6	.327	2.1	1B(119): -6.2, 3B(9): 0.4	2.9
2017	ARI	MLB	26	15	92	2.4	.200	0.0	1B(1): 0.0	0.0
2018	RNO	AAA	27	359	116	15.8	.351	-1.3	1B(64): 3.4, LF(18): -0.9	1.4
2018	ARI	MLB	27	53	59	-1.1	.200	0.2	1B(7): 0.2, LF(1): -0.1	-0.1
2019	ARI	MLB	28	603	112	19.4	.312	1.7	1B(142): 10.8	3.1
2020	ARI	MLB	29	567	110	19.0	.305	0.5	1B 4	2.4

Christian Walker, continued

Batted Ball Distribution

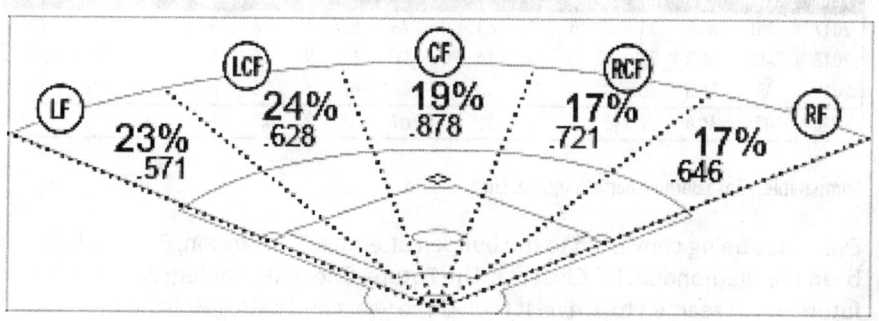

Strike Zone vs LHP

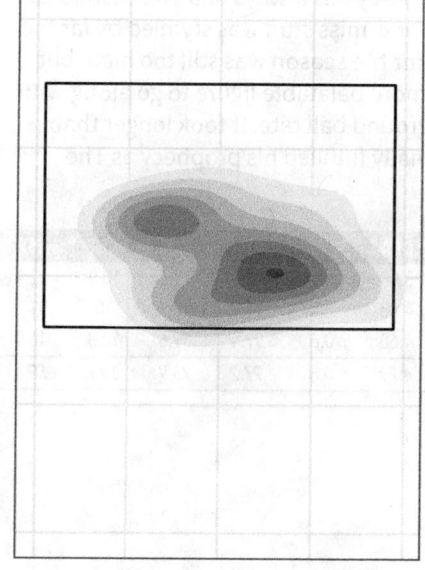

Strike Zone vs RHP

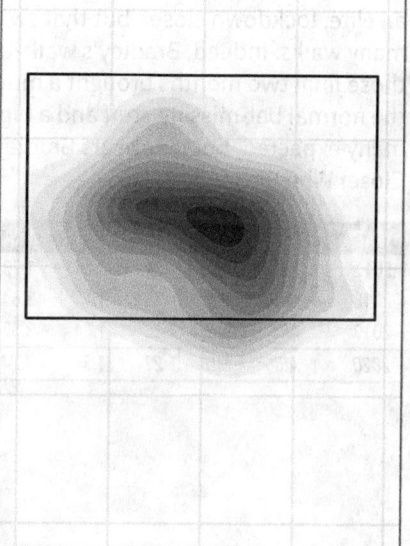

Arizona Diamondbacks 2020

Archie Bradley   RHP
Born: 08/10/92   Age: 27   Bats: R   Throws: R
Height: 6'4"   Weight: 225   Origin: Round 1, 2011 Draft (#7 overall)

YEAR	TEAM	LVL	AGE	W	L	SV	G	GS	IP	H	HR	BB/9	K/9	K	GB%	BABIP
2017	ARI	MLB	24	3	3	1	63	0	73	55	4	2.6	9.7	79	49%	.276
2018	ARI	MLB	25	4	5	3	76	0	71^2	62	9	2.5	9.4	75	50%	.282
2019	ARI	MLB	26	4	5	18	66	1	71^2	67	5	4.5	10.9	87	47%	.337
2020	ARI	MLB	27	3	3	32	58	0	61	57	7	4.1	9.9	67	48%	.311

Comparables: José Berríos, Aaron Sanchez, Lucas Giolito

Ever since being converted to the bullpen after the 2016 season, Bradley has been the Diamondbacks' Closer Of The Future. The only problem was that the future never seemed to arrive. It took three years and a Greg Holland implosion, but the future finally turned into the present in the second half of 2019. From the time he took over the job and earned his first save on July 30 through the end of the season, Bradley converted 18 of 19 save opportunities and allowed just six earned runs in 25 appearances. Bradley has always had The Stuff to be an elite, lockdown closer, but that swing-and-miss stuff was stymied by far too many walks. Indeed, Bradley's walk rate for the season was still too high, but those final two months brought a much more palatable figure to go along with the normal bat-missing stuff and a high ground ball rate. It took longer than many expected, but it appears Bradley finally fulfilled his prophecy as The Closer Who Was Promised.

YEAR	TEAM	LVL	AGE	WHIP	ERA	DRA	WARP	MPH	FB%	WHF	CSP
2017	ARI	MLB	24	1.04	1.73	3.88	1.1	98.3	75.6	10.9	52.7
2018	ARI	MLB	25	1.14	3.64	4.48	0.4	97.7	81.7	10	51.3
2019	ARI	MLB	26	1.44	3.52	4.60	0.6	97.4	69.6	10.8	46.9
2020	ARI	MLB	27	1.39	4.24	4.29	0.8	97.2	75.9	10.7	50.4

Archie Bradley, continued

Pitch Shape vs LHH
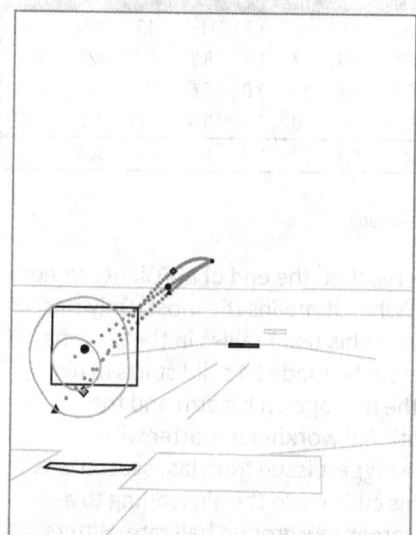

Pitch Shape vs RHH
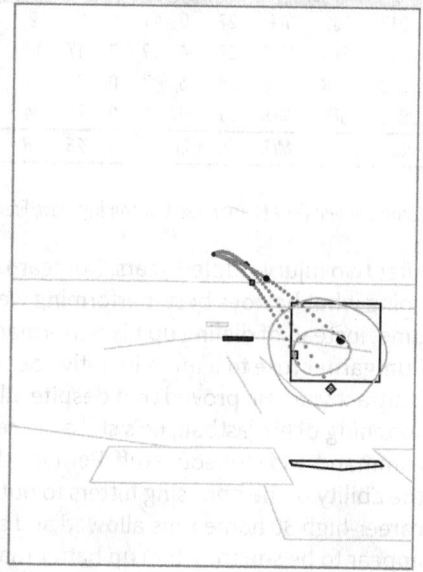

Type	Frequency	Velocity	H Movement	V Movement
● Fastball	58.3%	95.8 [110]	-7 [99]	-12.1 [110]
□ Sinker	11.3%	95.2 [113]	-12.3 [103]	-15.6 [117]
+ Cutter				
▲ Changeup	5.8%	88.7 [113]	-10.1 [105]	-23.4 [112]
✕ Splitter				
▽ Slider				
◇ Curveball	24.6%	82.3 [112]	3 [82]	-43.5 [109]
✜ Slow Curveball				
✳ Knuckleball				
▼ Screwball				

Arizona Diamondbacks 2020

Madison Bumgarner LHP
Born: 08/01/89 Age: 30 Bats: R Throws: L
Height: 6'4" Weight: 242 Origin: Round 1, 2007 Draft (#10 overall)

YEAR	TEAM	LVL	AGE	W	L	SV	G	GS	IP	H	HR	BB/9	K/9	K	GB%	BABIP
2017	SJO	A+	27	0	1	0	2	2	10	11	4	1.8	11.7	13	29%	.292
2017	SFN	MLB	27	4	9	0	17	17	111	101	17	1.6	8.2	101	42%	.272
2018	SFN	MLB	28	6	7	0	21	21	129^2	118	14	3.0	7.6	109	43%	.274
2019	SFN	MLB	29	9	9	0	34	34	207^2	191	30	1.9	8.8	203	37%	.289
2020	ARI	MLB	30	11	9	0	28	28	168	159	27	2.3	8.9	166	38%	.290

Comparables: Félix Hernández, Clayton Kershaw, Frank Tanana

After two injury-riddled years, Bumgarner reached the end of his Giants career doing what he does best: performing well when it means the most. Only this time, instead of dialing up his performance as his team rallies in the playoffs, Bumgarner rose to a more lucrative occasion: he made 34 solid starts in his contract year. He proved that despite all the mileage on his arm and the softening of his fastball, he's still an exceptional workhorse starter with command and strikeout stuff. Perhaps the biggest issue from last season was the ability of the opposing hitters to put his cutter into the air, leading to a career-high 30 home runs allowed and a career-low ground ball rate. Hitters appear to be squaring him up better than ever, but that didn't stop Arizona from bringing him across the division to be their new rotation cornerstone on a five-year contract.

YEAR	TEAM	LVL	AGE	WHIP	ERA	DRA	WARP	MPH	FB%	WHF	CSP
2017	SJO	A+	27	1.30	8.10	4.24	0.1				
2017	SFN	MLB	27	1.09	3.32	3.66	2.4	93.1	43	11.1	46
2018	SFN	MLB	28	1.24	3.26	4.47	1.3	92.4	34.4	10.1	49
2019	SFN	MLB	29	1.13	3.90	4.47	2.9	93.1	43.1	12.5	48.6
2020	ARI	MLB	30	1.20	3.92	4.19	3.0	92.2	40.5	11.5	48

Madison Bumgarner, continued

Pitch Shape vs LHH	Pitch Shape vs RHH
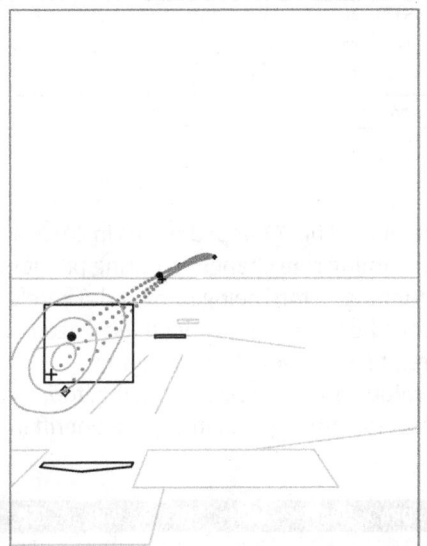	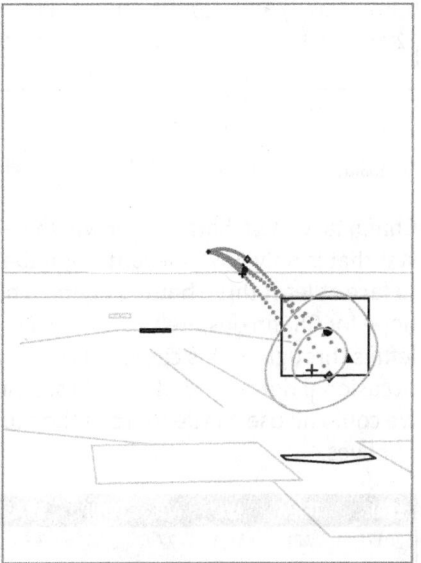

Type	Frequency	Velocity	H Movement	V Movement
● Fastball	43.0%	91.7 [98]	8.5 [93]	-15.2 [102]
☐ Sinker				
+ Cutter	33.3%	87.5 [93]	-0.6 [93]	-24.8 [97]
▲ Changeup	5.2%	84.5 [97]	12.2 [95]	-26.6 [102]
✕ Splitter				
▽ Slider				
◇ Curveball	18.3%	79 [101]	-9.7 [109]	-43.5 [109]
⊕ Slow Curveball				
✳ Knuckleball				
▼ Screwball				

Andrew Chafin LHP

Born: 06/17/90   Age: 30   Bats: R   Throws: L
Height: 6'2"   Weight: 225   Origin: Round 1, 2011 Draft (#43 overall)

YEAR	TEAM	LVL	AGE	W	L	SV	G	GS	IP	H	HR	BB/9	K/9	K	GB%	BABIP
2017	ARI	MLB	27	1	0	0	71	0	51^1	48	5	3.7	10.7	61	58%	.326
2018	ARI	MLB	28	1	6	0	77	0	49^1	41	0	4.6	9.7	53	51%	.313
2019	ARI	MLB	29	2	2	0	77	0	52^2	52	6	3.1	11.6	68	44%	.351
2020	ARI	MLB	30	3	3	2	53	0	56	49	6	3.7	10.8	67	48%	.311

Comparables: Neftalí Feliz, Luis Avilán, Jeremy Jeffress

Chafin faced two batters or fewer in nearly half of his 77 appearances in 2019, a stat that is only now relevant given the upcoming rule change requiring pitchers to face at least three batters or end a half-inning before being removed. There's hope for Chafin despite this, however: While he has primarily been used against lefties throughout his career, his splits aren't so extreme that facing the occasional right-handed bat will sap his value entirely. It's a good thing, too, as we could all use a little more of the mustachioed man nicknamed The Sheriff in our lives.

YEAR	TEAM	LVL	AGE	WHIP	ERA	DRA	WARP	MPH	FB%	WHF	CSP
2017	ARI	MLB	27	1.34	3.51	3.51	0.9	95.4	61.2	11.9	41.8
2018	ARI	MLB	28	1.34	3.10	4.23	0.4	95.7	56.6	14.7	42.7
2019	ARI	MLB	29	1.33	3.76	3.88	0.8	95.6	61.1	16.6	45.6
2020	ARI	MLB	30	1.30	3.68	3.80	1.0	94.8	59.5	14.7	43.6

Andrew Chafin, continued

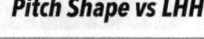
Pitch Shape vs LHH

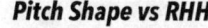
Pitch Shape vs RHH

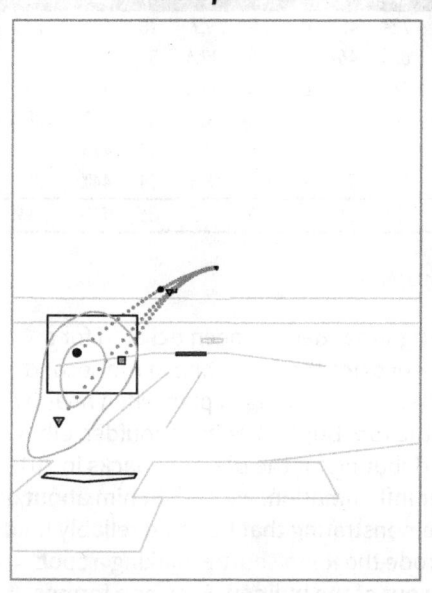
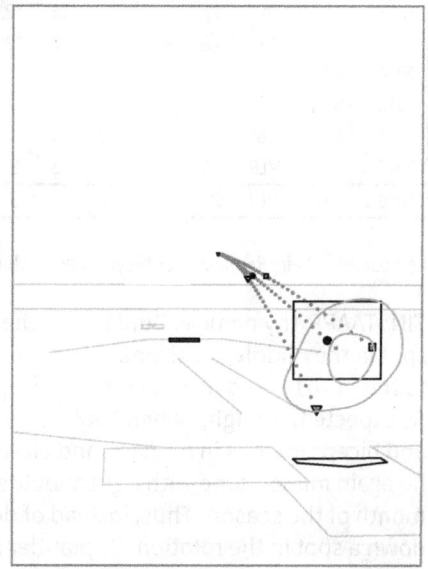

Type	Frequency	Velocity	H Movement	V Movement
● Fastball	32.3%	93.9 [104]	8.5 [93]	-14.5 [104]
□ Sinker	28.8%	94 [107]	13.4 [95]	-17.3 [111]
+ Cutter				
▲ Changeup				
✕ Splitter				
▽ Slider	38.9%	84.7 [101]	-0.1 [80]	-34.3 [96]
◇ Curveball				
⊕ Slow Curveball				
✷ Knuckleball				
▼ Screwball				

Arizona Diamondbacks 2020

Jon Duplantier RHP

Born: 07/11/94   Age: 25   Bats: L   Throws: R
Height: 6'4"   Weight: 225   Origin: Round 3, 2016 Draft (#89 overall)

YEAR	TEAM	LVL	AGE	W	L	SV	G	GS	IP	H	HR	BB/9	K/9	K	GB%	BABIP
2017	KNC	A	22	6	1	0	13	12	72^2	45	4	1.9	9.7	78	52%	.240
2017	VIS	A+	22	6	2	0	12	12	63^1	46	2	3.8	12.4	87	53%	.324
2018	DIA	RK	23	0	0	0	2	2	7	5	0	2.6	11.6	9	44%	.312
2018	WTN	AA	23	5	1	0	14	14	67	52	4	3.8	9.1	68	56%	.282
2019	RNO	AAA	24	1	2	0	13	11	38	31	1	6.6	10.4	44	47%	.323
2019	ARI	MLB	24	1	1	1	15	3	36^2	39	2	4.4	8.3	34	44%	.356
2020	ARI	MLB	25	2	2	0	30	3	42	44	6	4.5	7.5	35	46%	.299

Comparables: Yefry Ramírez, Alex Meyer, Jordan Montgomery

TINSTAAPP, thy name is Duplantier. The right-hander has been ticketed for a spot in the middle of Arizona's rotation ever since they took him in the second round in 2016, and he has certainly progressed according to plan when healthy. As expected, though, "when healthy" is the rub. Duplantier has shoulder, elbow, and biceps injuries in his past, and after debuting for the Diamondbacks in 2019 he again missed time with right shoulder inflammation, which cost him about a month of the season. Thus, instead of demonstrating that he could reliably hold down a spot in the rotation, Duplantier rode the Reno shuttle, making a spot start here and there, but mostly pitching out of the bullpen. Even as a former top pitching prospect in the system, Duplantier's ceiling was never much beyond "future rotation piece who could peak higher if everything went right." Injury concerns, however, could relegate him to more of a "swingman who we never know if we can rely on" type of role.

YEAR	TEAM	LVL	AGE	WHIP	ERA	DRA	WARP	MPH	FB%	WHF	CSP
2017	KNC	A	22	0.83	1.24	2.23	2.6				
2017	VIS	A+	22	1.15	1.56	3.49	1.3				
2018	DIA	RK	23	1.00	1.29	3.05	0.2				
2018	WTN	AA	23	1.19	2.69	3.79	1.2				
2019	RNO	AAA	24	1.55	5.21	2.93	1.4				
2019	ARI	MLB	24	1.55	4.42	5.73	-0.1	94.3	59	9.2	47.9
2020	ARI	MLB	25	1.54	5.22	5.14	0.2	94.0	60.4	9.4	49

Jon Duplantier, continued

Pitch Shape vs LHH

Pitch Shape vs RHH

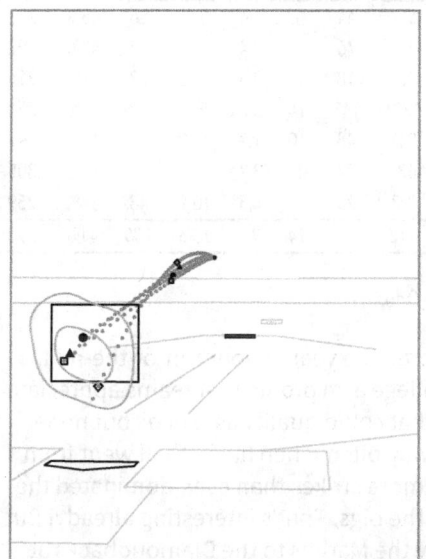 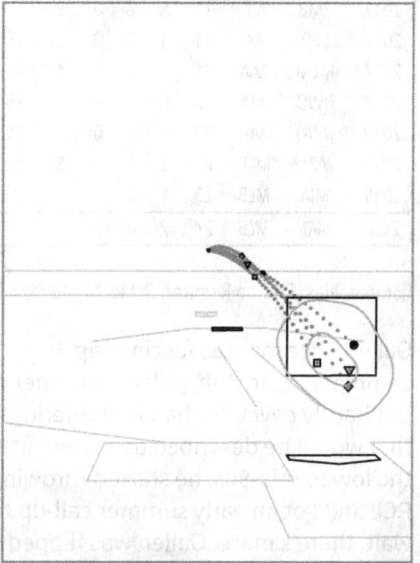

Type	Frequency	Velocity	H Movement	V Movement
● Fastball	29.0%	92.6 [101]	-6.1 [103]	-14.2 [105]
☐ Sinker	29.9%	92.4 [99]	-13.7 [93]	-19 [105]
✚ Cutter				
▲ Changeup	9.0%	84.4 [97]	-13.8 [88]	-29.4 [94]
✕ Splitter				
▽ Slider	19.4%	83.8 [97]	5.9 [104]	-34.5 [96]
◇ Curveball	12.6%	78.8 [101]	8.6 [105]	-50.7 [93]
✦ Slow Curveball				
✱ Knuckleball				
▼ Screwball				

Arizona Diamondbacks 2020

Zac Gallen RHP
Born: 08/03/95   Age: 24   Bats: R   Throws: R
Height: 6'2"   Weight: 191   Origin: Round 3, 2016 Draft (#106 overall)

YEAR	TEAM	LVL	AGE	W	L	SV	G	GS	IP	H	HR	BB/9	K/9	K	GB%	BABIP
2017	PMB	A+	21	5	2	0	9	9	55.2	44	1	1.6	9.1	56	48%	.283
2017	SFD	AA	21	4	5	0	13	13	71.1	76	8	2.4	5.3	42	42%	.292
2017	MEM	AAA	21	1	1	0	4	4	20.2	18	2	2.6	10.0	23	47%	.314
2018	NWO	AAA	22	8	9	0	25	25	133.1	148	14	3.2	9.2	136	41%	.351
2019	NWO	AAA	23	9	1	0	14	14	91.1	48	10	1.7	11.0	112	48%	.197
2019	ARI	MLB	23	2	3	0	8	8	43.2	37	5	3.7	10.9	53	44%	.305
2019	MIA	MLB	23	1	3	0	7	7	36.1	25	3	4.5	10.7	43	34%	.259
2020	ARI	MLB	24	7	6	0	21	21	112	95	14	3.3	10.5	130	41%	.293

Comparables: Erasmo Ramírez, Rafael Montero, Jake Odorizzi

Gallen's season was fascinating. He entered the year as your run-of-the-mill, command over stuff, polished former college arm profile that teams appreciate but hardly covet. He had four offerings that could qualify as "solid" but none that would be described as a true put-away pitch. Then his fastball went from the low to mid-90s, he started throwing more strikes than ever, dominated the PCL and got an early summer call-up to the bigs. That's interesting already! But wait, there's more. Gallen was flipped by the Marlins to the Diamondbacks at the trade deadline for Jazz Chisholm in one of those rare prospect-for-prospect challenge trades that harkens memories of Matt Garza and Delmon Young. He continued to shove in Arizona, and now looks the part of a solid No. 3 in a good rotation, with a shot to climb even higher. What a difference a year can make.

YEAR	TEAM	LVL	AGE	WHIP	ERA	DRA	WARP	MPH	FB%	WHF	CSP
2017	PMB	A+	21	0.97	1.62	3.31	1.3				
2017	SFD	AA	21	1.33	3.79	4.43	0.6				
2017	MEM	AAA	21	1.16	3.48	3.24	0.6				
2018	NWO	AAA	22	1.47	3.64	5.03	0.8				
2019	NWO	AAA	23	0.71	1.77	0.79	5.2				
2019	ARI	MLB	23	1.26	2.89	3.43	1.1	95.5	50.7	14	45.6
2019	MIA	MLB	23	1.18	2.72	4.34	0.6	94.7	48.3	12.7	45.1
2020	ARI	MLB	24	1.22	3.48	3.67	2.6	94.9	51.1	13.8	46.7

Zac Gallen, continued

Pitch Shape vs LHH

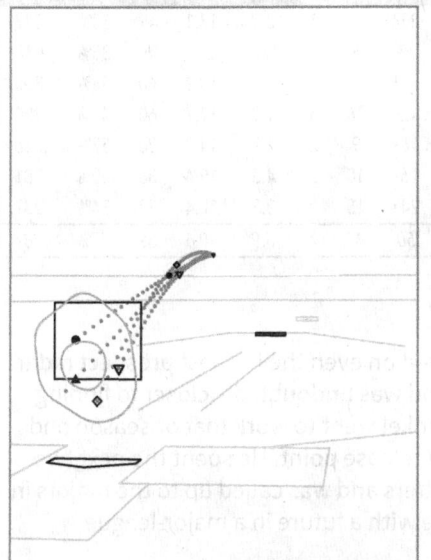

Pitch Shape vs RHH

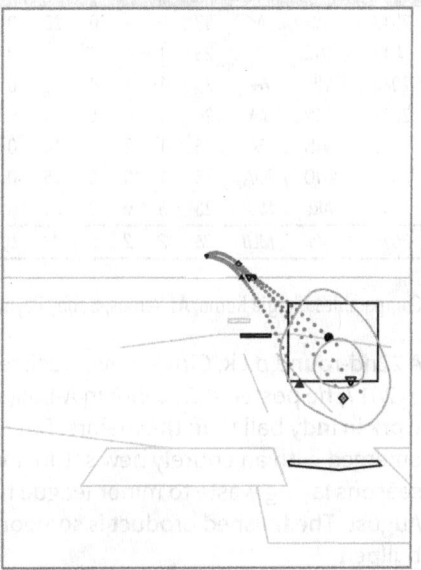

Type	Frequency	Velocity	H Movement	V Movement
● Fastball	47.5%	93.1 [102]	-4.6 [110]	-12.9 [108]
☐ Sinker				
+ Cutter				
▲ Changeup	16.0%	85.2 [100]	-10.2 [105]	-29.2 [95]
✕ Splitter				
▽ Slider	15.4%	87.2 [112]	6.4 [106]	-29.1 [112]
◇ Curveball	19.0%	79.4 [102]	8.3 [103]	-48.2 [99]
✦ Slow Curveball				
✱ Knuckleball				
▼ Screwball				

Arizona Diamondbacks 2020

Kevin Ginkel   RHP
Born: 03/24/94   Age: 26   Bats: L   Throws: R
Height: 6'4"   Weight: 210   Origin: Round 22, 2016 Draft (#659 overall)

YEAR	TEAM	LVL	AGE	W	L	SV	G	GS	IP	H	HR	BB/9	K/9	K	GB%	BABIP
2017	YAK	A-	23	0	1	0	20	0	33²	26	1	2.9	13.1	49	38%	.347
2017	KNC	A	23	1	1	0	6	0	6²	8	1	12.1	6.8	5	35%	.318
2018	VIS	A+	24	1	1	4	20	0	27¹	20	2	1.0	13.2	40	38%	.305
2018	WTN	AA	24	5	0	5	34	0	42²	26	3	1.9	12.7	60	40%	.258
2019	WTN	AA	25	1	2	5	14	0	16²	9	2	2.7	14.0	26	52%	.226
2019	RNO	AAA	25	1	0	6	15	0	16²	10	2	4.3	19.4	36	39%	.381
2019	ARI	MLB	25	3	0	2	25	0	24¹	15	2	3.3	10.4	28	34%	.232
2020	ARI	MLB	26	2	2	2	47	0	50	43	7	3.9	10.6	59	37%	.287

Comparables: Sergio Romo, AJ Ramos, Bobby Poyner

A 22nd-round pick, Ginkel never registered on even the keenest prospect radar. In 2017, he posted a 5.36 ERA in A-ball and was undoubtedly closer to finding work in Indy ball than the majors. But Ginkel went to work that offseason and emerged with an entirely new setup and release point. He spent the next two seasons laying waste to minor league hitters and was called up to the majors in August. The finished product is someone with a future in a major-league bullpen.

YEAR	TEAM	LVL	AGE	WHIP	ERA	DRA	WARP	MPH	FB%	WHF	CSP
2017	YAK	A-	23	1.10	3.48	3.90	0.4				
2017	KNC	A	23	2.55	14.85	8.20	-0.3				
2018	VIS	A+	24	0.84	0.99	1.92	1.0				
2018	WTN	AA	24	0.82	1.69	2.30	1.3				
2019	WTN	AA	25	0.84	2.16	2.42	0.4				
2019	RNO	AAA	25	1.08	1.62	1.51	0.8				
2019	ARI	MLB	25	0.99	1.48	3.80	0.4	95.3	54	15.4	42.5
2020	ARI	MLB	26	1.28	3.90	4.07	0.7	94.9	55	15.7	43.3

Kevin Ginkel, continued

Pitch Shape vs LHH

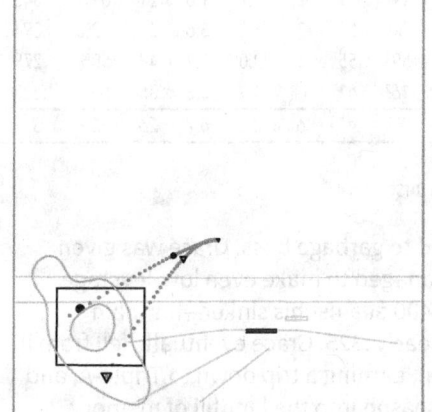

Pitch Shape vs RHH

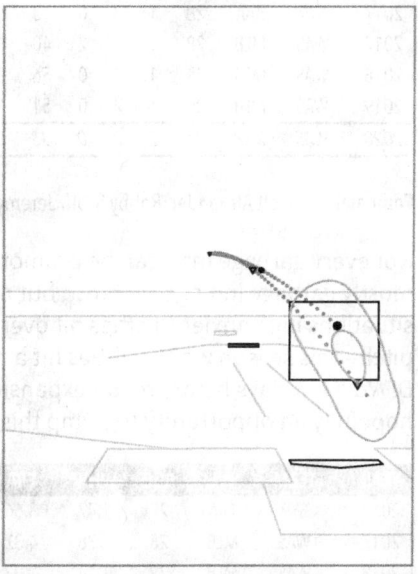

Type	Frequency	Velocity	H Movement	V Movement
● Fastball	54.0%	93.6 [103]	-8.6 [92]	-15 [103]
☐ Sinker				
+ Cutter				
▲ Changeup				
✕ Splitter				
▽ Slider	44.9%	83.6 [96]	2.4 [89]	-35.9 [92]
◇ Curveball				
⊕ Slow Curveball				
✱ Knuckleball				
▼ Screwball				

Arizona Diamondbacks 2020

Matt Grace LHP
Born: 12/14/88 Age: 31 Bats: L Throws: L
Height: 6'4" Weight: 215 Origin: Round 8, 2010 Draft (#236 overall)

YEAR	TEAM	LVL	AGE	W	L	SV	G	GS	IP	H	HR	BB/9	K/9	K	GB%	BABIP
2017	SYR	AAA	28	1	3	0	13	1	19^2	21	2	3.7	9.6	21	61%	.345
2017	WAS	MLB	28	1	0	2	40	1	50	50	3	3.2	5.6	31	63%	.294
2018	WAS	MLB	29	1	1	0	56	0	59^2	55	5	2.0	7.2	48	50%	.279
2019	WAS	MLB	30	1	2	0	51	1	46^2	61	11	1.9	6.8	35	50%	.338
2020	WAS	MLB	31	2	2	0	33	0	35	41	6	2.6	6.7	26	52%	.317

Comparables: Scott Alexander, Robby Scott, Jeremy Horst

Not every garbage man can be promoted to garbage boss. Grace was given mostly garbage innings to throw, but managed to make even low-leverage situations high anxiety. Lefties hit over .400 against his sinker—his main pitch—this season while righties hit a measly .325. Grace eventually fell from it, DFA'd a few days before roster expansion, earning a trip down to Triple-A, and hopefully an opportunity to dump this season into the landfill of memory.

YEAR	TEAM	LVL	AGE	WHIP	ERA	DRA	WARP	MPH	FB%	WHF	CSP
2017	SYR	AAA	28	1.47	3.66	4.60	0.2				
2017	WAS	MLB	28	1.36	4.32	6.01	-0.5	92.8	72.2	7.9	50.9
2018	WAS	MLB	29	1.14	2.87	4.45	0.3	93.1	66.9	8.3	54.6
2019	WAS	MLB	30	1.52	6.36	5.96	-0.3	93.0	61.9	9.3	50.3
2020	WAS	MLB	31	1.45	5.16	5.26	0.1	92.2	65.9	8.5	51.6

Matt Grace, continued

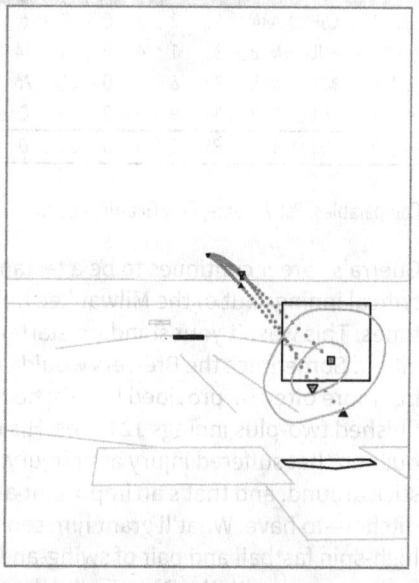

Type	Frequency	Velocity	H Movement	V Movement
● Fastball				
☐ Sinker	61.6%	91.6 [95]	13 [98]	-22.6 [92]
+ Cutter				
▲ Changeup	4.7%	86.1 [103]	14.7 [84]	-27.9 [99]
✕ Splitter				
▽ Slider	30.5%	83.7 [97]	-3.4 [93]	-32.7 [101]
◇ Curveball				
⊕ Slow Curveball				
✱ Knuckleball				
▼ Screwball				

Arizona Diamondbacks 2020

Junior Guerra RHP

Born: 01/16/85 Age: 35 Bats: R Throws: R
Height: 6'0" Weight: 205 Origin: International Free Agent, 2001

YEAR	TEAM	LVL	AGE	W	L	SV	G	GS	IP	H	HR	BB/9	K/9	K	GB%	BABIP
2017	CSP	AAA	32	2	2	0	6	6	30	27	0	3.6	6.0	20	47%	.303
2017	MIL	MLB	32	1	4	0	21	14	70^1	61	18	5.5	8.6	67	36%	.236
2018	MIL	MLB	33	6	9	0	31	26	141	143	19	3.5	8.7	136	45%	.313
2019	MIL	MLB	34	9	5	3	72	0	83^2	58	11	3.9	8.3	77	46%	.218
2020	ARI	MLB	35	3	3	0	53	0	56	50	9	4.0	8.7	54	46%	.276

Comparables: Pat Venditte, Cory Gearrin, Aquilino Lopez

Guerra's career continues to be a testament to the value of versatility. He ate critical innings out of the Milwaukee bullpen in 2019, just a year after starting 26 times. This wasn't your standard starter-to-middle-reliever conversion tale, either. Sometimes the Brewers would call on him to get past one right-hander, but more often he provided length: he recorded at least four outs 23 times, and finished two-plus innings 12 times. His reliability was critical for a Brewers bullpen that suffered injury after injury. Guerra has shown he will do anything to stick around, and that's an important attribute for any player—particularly a pitcher—to have. What'll grant him senior status is his ability to maintain his high-spin fastball and pair of swing-and-miss secondaries. Unfortunately, it'll have to come with the Diamondbacks organization, as the Brewers non-tendered Guerra after the season.

YEAR	TEAM	LVL	AGE	WHIP	ERA	DRA	WARP	MPH	FB%	WHF	CSP
2017	CSP	AAA	32	1.30	2.10	3.55	0.7				
2017	MIL	MLB	32	1.48	5.12	6.31	-0.6	94.3	64.8	11.8	41.4
2018	MIL	MLB	33	1.40	4.09	4.50	1.3	95.4	69	11.6	46.5
2019	MIL	MLB	34	1.12	3.55	4.04	1.2	96.4	60.2	12	45.1
2020	ARI	MLB	35	1.34	4.21	4.34	0.7	94.3	64	11.6	43.9

Junior Guerra, continued

Pitch Shape vs LHH

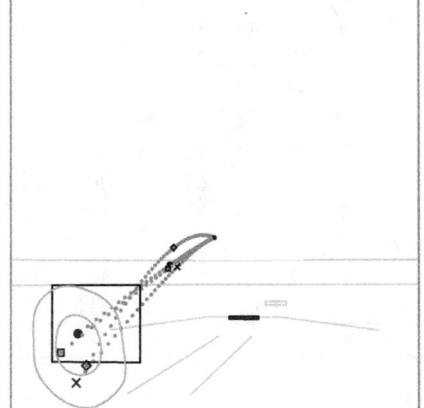

Pitch Shape vs RHH

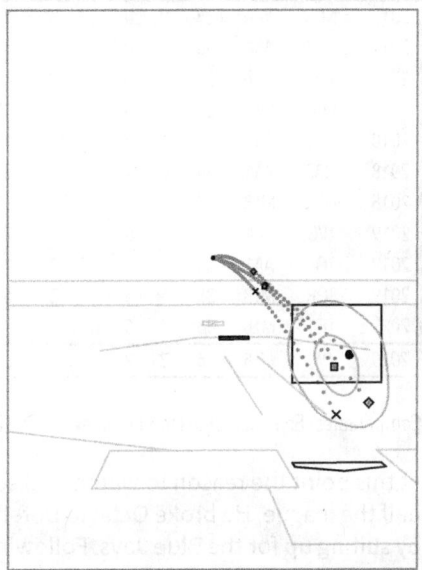

Type	Frequency	Velocity	H Movement	V Movement
● Fastball	31.2%	94.9 [107]	-5.5 [106]	-10.8 [113]
□ Sinker	29.0%	95.2 [113]	-12.4 [102]	-15 [119]
+ Cutter				
▲ Changeup				
× Splitter	20.8%	86.4 [106]	-7.5 [102]	-23.6 [118]
▽ Slider				
◇ Curveball	18.3%	82.4 [113]	6.8 [97]	-42.9 [110]
⊕ Slow Curveball				
✱ Knuckleball				
▼ Screwball				

Arizona Diamondbacks 2020

Edwin Jackson RHP

Born: 09/09/83   Age: 36   Bats: R   Throws: R
Height: 6'2"   Weight: 215   Origin: Round 6, 2001 Draft (#190 overall)

YEAR	TEAM	LVL	AGE	W	L	SV	G	GS	IP	H	HR	BB/9	K/9	K	GB%	BABIP
2017	NOR	AAA	33	0	0	2	12	1	20^1	20	1	4.4	7.5	17	33%	.339
2017	SYR	AAA	33	2	0	0	5	4	20^1	9	0	4.4	9.7	22	51%	.191
2017	BAL	MLB	33	0	0	0	3	0	5	11	2	7.2	3.6	2	30%	.429
2017	WAS	MLB	33	5	6	0	13	13	71	75	18	3.2	7.4	58	40%	.273
2018	SYR	AAA	34	4	2	0	10	10	55^2	51	4	3.6	7.6	47	42%	.285
2018	NAS	AAA	34	0	1	0	3	3	15^2	12	1	4.6	9.2	16	41%	.256
2018	OAK	MLB	34	6	3	0	17	17	92	75	12	3.6	6.7	68	38%	.240
2019	LVG	AAA	35	0	0	0	2	2	9^2	9	3	6.5	9.3	10	54%	.240
2019	TOL	AAA	35	0	2	0	2	2	7^2	11	1	4.7	2.3	2	38%	.385
2019	TOR	MLB	35	1	5	0	8	5	28^1	49	12	4.1	6.0	19	44%	.378
2019	DET	MLB	35	2	5	0	10	8	39^1	56	11	4.3	7.6	33	43%	.352
2020	DET	MLB	36	2	2	0	33	0	35	40	7	4.2	7.2	28	42%	.308

Comparables: Ervin Santana, Homer Bailey, Gavin Floyd

At this point the reason to watch Jackson is to see if he'll end up representing half the league. He broke Octavio Dotel's record for teams played with last year by suiting up for the Blue Jays. Following a midseason release, he double-dipped with the Tigers, the org with which he earned his lone All-Star nod, rather than latching on with team No. 15. This could be the year, though, and the more words reserved for describing his uniform quantity, the less needed to describe his pitching quality.

YEAR	TEAM	LVL	AGE	WHIP	ERA	DRA	WARP	MPH	FB%	WHF	CSP
2017	NOR	AAA	33	1.48	3.10	4.83	0.2				
2017	SYR	AAA	33	0.93	0.44	4.80	0.2				
2017	BAL	MLB	33	3.00	7.20	8.81	-0.2	93.9	76.9	8.3	42.3
2017	WAS	MLB	33	1.41	5.07	6.39	-0.7	95.8	76.9	10.9	48
2018	SYR	AAA	34	1.31	3.40	4.50	0.7				
2018	NAS	AAA	34	1.28	4.02	3.45	0.4				
2018	OAK	MLB	34	1.22	3.33	5.23	0.1	95.7	67	9.7	44.4
2019	LVG	AAA	35	1.66	8.38	5.85	0.1				
2019	TOL	AAA	35	1.96	5.87	5.73	0.1				
2019	TOR	MLB	35	2.19	11.12	10.20	-1.4	95.8	64.9	9.6	45
2019	DET	MLB	35	1.91	8.47	9.31	-1.5	95.6	64.9	11.8	47.3
2020	DET	MLB	36	1.61	6.24	5.93	-0.3	94.3	67	10.2	45

Edwin Jackson, continued

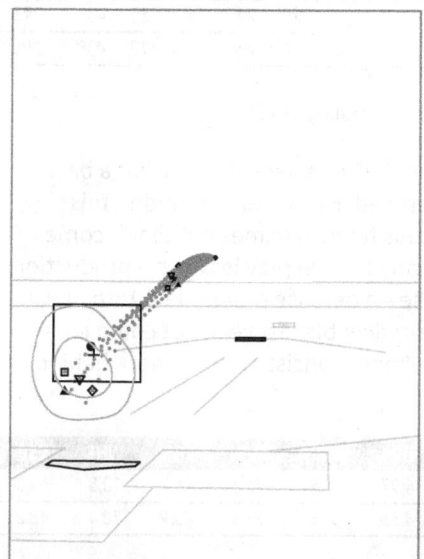

Pitch Shape vs LHH

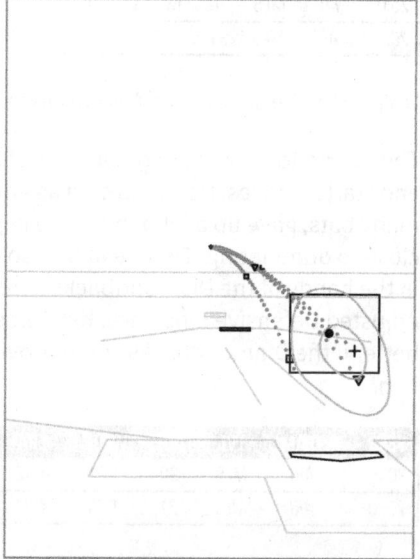

Pitch Shape vs RHH

Type		Frequency	Velocity	H Movement	V Movement
●	Fastball	21.3%	93.5 [103]	-4 [113]	-15.8 [100]
□	Sinker	17.3%	93.6 [105]	-11.2 [109]	-17.5 [110]
+	Cutter	26.5%	91.8 [120]	0.2 [91]	-21 [112]
▲	Changeup	6.8%	87 [106]	-14 [87]	-21.4 [117]
✕	Splitter				
▽	Slider	25.0%	86 [107]	3 [92]	-31.9 [103]
◇	Curveball	3.0%	78.4 [99]	5.1 [90]	-46.3 [103]
⊕	Slow Curveball				
✱	Knuckleball				
▼	Screwball				

Merrill Kelly RHP

Born: 10/14/88 Age: 31 Bats: R Throws: R
Height: 6'2" Weight: 190 Origin: Round 8, 2010 Draft (#251 overall)

YEAR	TEAM	LVL	AGE	W	L	SV	G	GS	IP	H	HR	BB/9	K/9	K	GB%	BABIP
2019	ARI	MLB	30	13	14	0	32	32	183^1	184	29	2.8	7.8	158	43%	.293
2020	ARI	MLB	31	8	9	0	24	24	139	142	22	2.9	7.7	118	43%	.298

Comparables: Brandon Cumpton, Asher Wojciechowski, Taylor Jungmann

The Diamondbacks signed Kelly out of the KBO to a deal akin to what a back-end starter makes. He performed as advertised. He ate innings, didn't miss many bats, gave up a lot of hits, and kept his team in games but didn't come close to dominating. That he allows so many balls in play leaves his production in the hands of the Diamondbacks defense—a defense that ranked 18th in Park Adjusted Defensive Efficiency. Kelly was serviceable last year, but could look better if the Diamondbacks could provide more consistent glovework behind him.

YEAR	TEAM	LVL	AGE	WHIP	ERA	DRA	WARP	MPH	FB%	WHF	CSP
2019	ARI	MLB	30	1.31	4.42	4.97	1.6	94.2	46.2	10.5	48.5
2020	ARI	MLB	31	1.35	4.51	4.66	1.8	93.4	45.9	10.4	48.2

Merrill Kelly, continued

Pitch Shape vs LHH

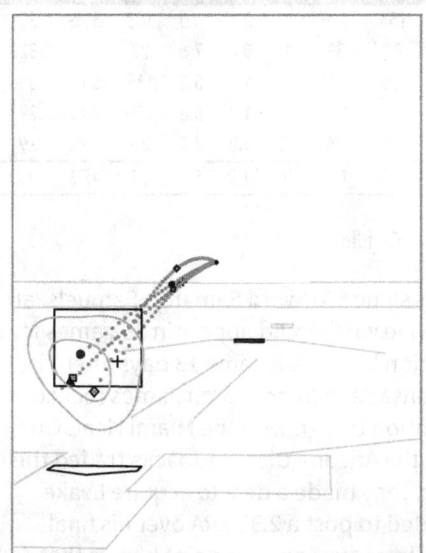

Pitch Shape vs RHH

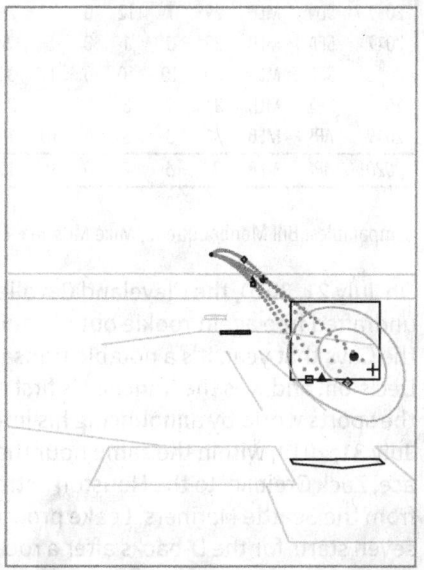

Type	Frequency	Velocity	H Movement	V Movement
● Fastball	36.0%	92.3 [100]	-3.9 [113]	-15 [102]
□ Sinker	10.2%	91.8 [96]	-11.9 [105]	-21.3 [97]
+ Cutter	19.2%	90.2 [110]	2 [101]	-20.2 [114]
▲ Changeup	13.2%	86.3 [104]	-10.9 [101]	-21.1 [118]
✕ Splitter				
▽ Slider				
◇ Curveball	21.4%	80.8 [107]	8.7 [105]	-48.7 [98]
✦ Slow Curveball				
✳ Knuckleball				
▼ Screwball				

Arizona Diamondbacks 2020

Mike Leake RHP

Born: 11/12/87 Age: 32 Bats: R Throws: R
Height: 5'10" Weight: 170 Origin: Round 1, 2009 Draft (#8 overall)

YEAR	TEAM	LVL	AGE	W	L	SV	G	GS	IP	H	HR	BB/9	K/9	K	GB%	BABIP
2017	SLN	MLB	29	7	12	0	26	26	154	169	19	2.0	6.0	103	55%	.306
2017	SEA	MLB	29	3	1	0	5	5	32	32	1	0.6	7.6	27	50%	.323
2018	SEA	MLB	30	10	10	0	31	31	185^2	207	23	1.6	5.8	119	50%	.306
2019	SEA	MLB	31	9	8	0	22	22	137	153	26	1.2	6.6	100	48%	.297
2019	ARI	MLB	31	3	3	0	10	10	60	74	15	1.2	4.1	27	46%	.291
2020	ARI	MLB	32	6	7	0	19	19	103	118	18	1.8	5.8	66	47%	.300

Comparables: Bill Monbouquette, Mike Mussina, Frank Castillo

On July 21, 2010, the Cleveland Cavaliers signed forward Samardo Samuels, an undrafted free agent rookie out of Louisville who would appear in 36 games for the Cavs that year. It's a notable transaction because it came 13 days after The Decision, and was the franchise's first transaction after LeBron James rocked the sports world by announcing his intention to sign with the Miami Heat. On July 31, 2019, within the same hour that the Arizona Diamondbacks traded their ace, Zack Greinke, to the Houston Astros, they made a deal to acquire Leake from the Seattle Mariners. Leake proceeded to post a 2.33 ERA over his final seven starts for the D-backs after a rocky introduction. The point here is that there are worse ways to replace a departed star.

YEAR	TEAM	LVL	AGE	WHIP	ERA	DRA	WARP	MPH	FB%	WHF	CSP
2017	SLN	MLB	29	1.32	4.21	4.20	2.4	92.1	58.1	8.5	48.8
2017	SEA	MLB	29	1.06	2.53	3.64	0.7	92.3	58.1	9.7	47.9
2018	SEA	MLB	30	1.30	4.36	4.46	1.8	91.0	59.4	8.3	50.7
2019	SEA	MLB	31	1.26	4.27	5.87	-0.2	90.4	57.5	9.2	51.2
2019	ARI	MLB	31	1.37	4.35	9.04	-2.1	90.5	57.5	9.2	50.9
2020	ARI	MLB	32	1.34	4.92	5.09	0.9	90.1	57.8	8.7	49.9

Mike Leake, continued

Pitch Shape vs LHH

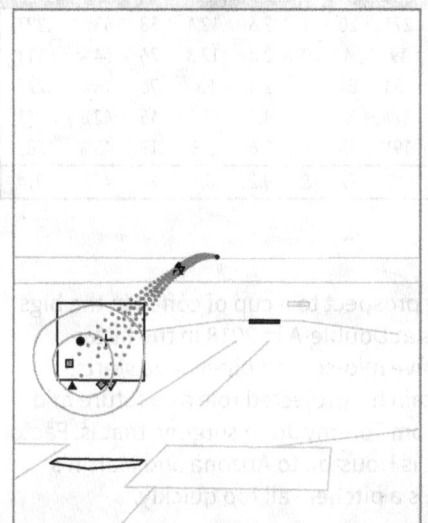

Pitch Shape vs RHH

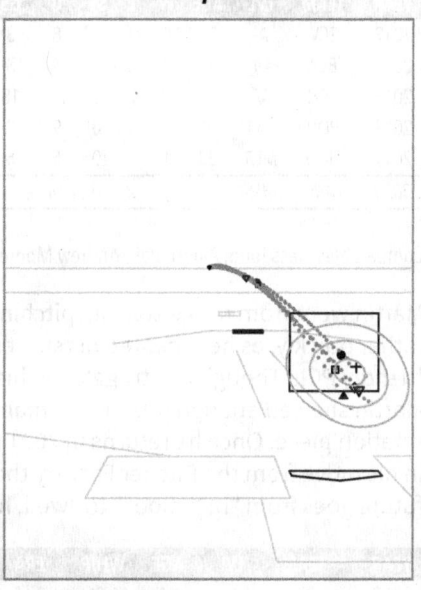

Type	Frequency	Velocity	H Movement	V Movement
● Fastball	9.5%	89 [90]	-6 [104]	-23.5 [80]
☐ Sinker	23.0%	88.5 [79]	-9.4 [121]	-27.3 [76]
+ Cutter	26.0%	87 [89]	1.7 [99]	-27 [89]
▲ Changeup	20.8%	84.4 [97]	-10.4 [103]	-35.7 [76]
✕ Splitter				
▽ Slider	16.4%	80.4 [83]	9.7 [120]	-38.9 [83]
◇ Curveball	4.4%	79.4 [103]	11.1 [115]	-41.3 [113]
✢ Slow Curveball				
✳ Knuckleball				
▼ Screwball				

Arizona Diamondbacks 2020

Corbin Martin RHP

Born: 12/28/95 Age: 24 Bats: R Throws: R
Height: 6'2" Weight: 200 Origin: Round 2, 2017 Draft (#56 overall)

YEAR	TEAM	LVL	AGE	W	L	SV	G	GS	IP	H	HR	BB/9	K/9	K	GB%	BABIP
2017	TCV	A-	21	0	1	1	8	3	27²	20	1	2.6	12.4	38	63%	.297
2018	BCA	A+	22	2	0	1	4	3	19	4	0	3.3	12.3	26	64%	.111
2018	CCH	AA	22	7	2	0	21	18	103	84	7	2.4	8.4	96	48%	.277
2019	ROU	AAA	23	2	1	0	9	8	37¹	33	2	4.3	10.8	45	42%	.341
2019	HOU	MLB	23	1	1	0	5	5	19¹	23	8	5.6	8.8	19	43%	.283
2020	ARI	MLB	24	1	2	0	14	3	24	27	5	4.2	8.1	22	42%	.314

Comparables: Jess Todd, Aaron Blair, Andrew Moore

Martin went from fringe starting pitching prospect to a cup of coffee in the bigs rather quickly, as he repeated his success at Double-A in 2018 in the hitter-friendly PCL. Though he struggled in his five mid-season big-league starts, Martin showed enough promise to maintain his projected role as a future mid-rotation piece. Once he returns in 2021 from Tommy John surgery, that is. Factor in his move from the Pitcher Factory that is Houston to Arizona and Martin's future goes from "high floor" to "well, he's a pitcher" all too quickly.

YEAR	TEAM	LVL	AGE	WHIP	ERA	DRA	WARP	MPH	FB%	WHF	CSP
2017	TCV	A-	21	1.01	2.60	2.42	0.8				
2018	BCA	A+	22	0.58	0.00	1.74	0.8				
2018	CCH	AA	22	1.09	2.97	3.34	2.3				
2019	ROU	AAA	23	1.37	3.13	3.00	1.3				
2019	HOU	MLB	23	1.81	5.59	7.18	-0.3	97.3	62.6	9.4	43.0
2020	ARI	MLB	24	1.60	6.03	5.88	-0.1	97.1	64.5	9.7	45.2

Corbin Martin, continued

Pitch Shape vs LHH

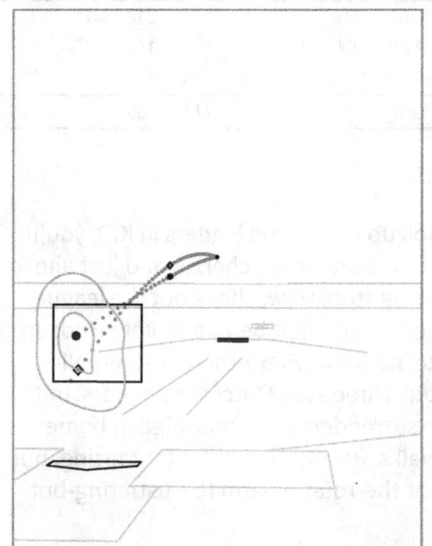

Pitch Shape vs RHH

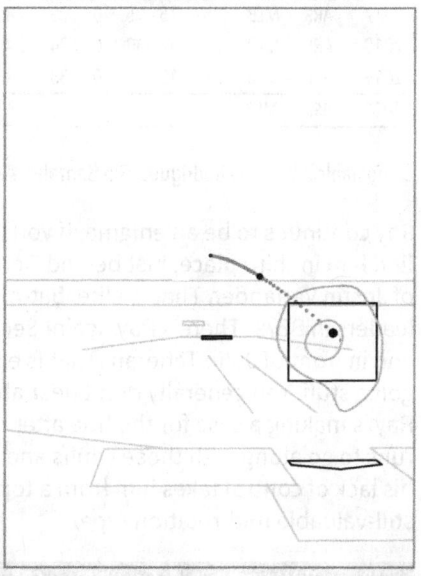

Type	Frequency	Velocity	H Movement	V Movement
● Fastball	62.6%	95.4 [109]	-4.6 [110]	-12.9 [108]
☐ Sinker				
+ Cutter				
▲ Changeup	11.0%	87.5 [108]	-14.2 [86]	-28.6 [97]
✕ Splitter				
▽ Slider	7.3%	89.1 [120]	4.6 [98]	-27.2 [117]
◇ Curveball	19.1%	83.7 [117]	9.1 [107]	-40.5 [115]
⊕ Slow Curveball				
✳ Knuckleball				
▼ Screwball				

Arizona Diamondbacks 2020

Robbie Ray LHP
Born: 10/01/91 Age: 28 Bats: L Throws: L
Height: 6'2" Weight: 195 Origin: Round 12, 2010 Draft (#356 overall)

YEAR	TEAM	LVL	AGE	W	L	SV	G	GS	IP	H	HR	BB/9	K/9	K	GB%	BABIP
2017	ARI	MLB	25	15	5	0	28	28	162	116	23	3.9	12.1	218	42%	.267
2018	ARI	MLB	26	6	2	0	24	24	123²	97	19	5.1	12.0	165	41%	.292
2019	ARI	MLB	27	12	8	0	33	33	174¹	150	30	4.3	12.1	235	41%	.306
2020	ARI	MLB	28	9	8	0	26	26	137	113	21	4.2	11.8	180	40%	.293

Comparables: Eduardo Rodriguez, Gio Gonzalez, A.J. Cole

Ray continues to be an enigma. If you look up the league leaders in K/9, you'll find him in third place, just behind Gerrit Cole and Max Scherzer and just ahead of Justin Verlander. That is elite, bat-missing stuff. Now, check out the league leaders in BB/9. There's Ray again! Second place, right behind Dakota Hudson and in front of Julio Teheran. That is elite, no-idea-where-the-hell-the-ball-is-going stuff. You generally don't hear about Three True Outcome pitchers, but Ray is making a case for the title after he surrendered a career-high in home runs to go along with those whiffs and walks. Ray's pure stuff is tantalizing, but his lack of control takes him from a top-of-the-rotation arm to frustrating-but-still-valuable mid-rotation type.

YEAR	TEAM	LVL	AGE	WHIP	ERA	DRA	WARP	MPH	FB%	WHF	CSP
2017	ARI	MLB	25	1.15	2.89	3.06	4.6	96.5	59.3	15.3	44.2
2018	ARI	MLB	26	1.35	3.93	3.99	1.9	96.2	53.9	13.8	44.8
2019	ARI	MLB	27	1.34	4.34	4.09	3.2	94.6	52.8	14.8	45.4
2020	ARI	MLB	28	1.29	3.85	3.98	2.8	95.0	55	14.7	45.2

Robbie Ray, continued

Pitch Shape vs LHH
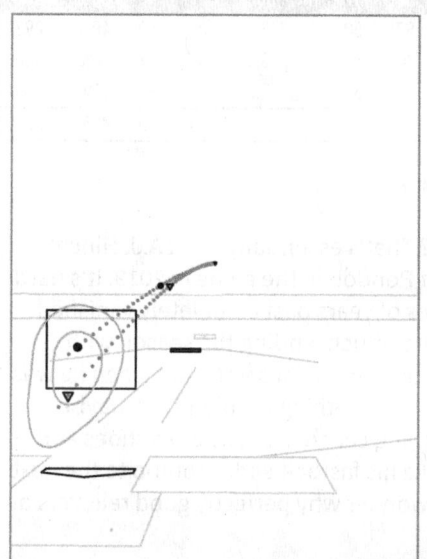

Pitch Shape vs RHH
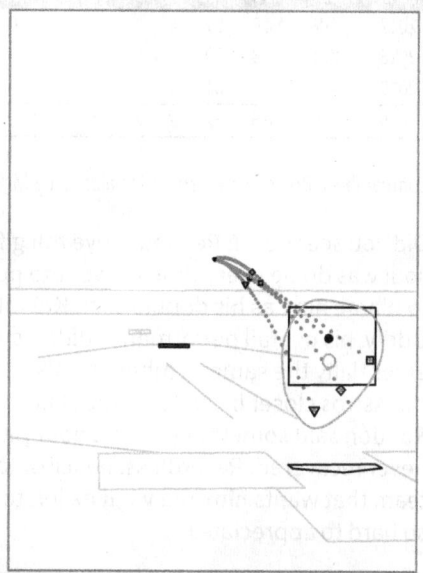

Type	Frequency	Velocity	H Movement	V Movement
● Fastball	43.7%	92.7 [101]	6.6 [101]	-12.4 [109]
☐ Sinker	9.1%	92.3 [99]	12.7 [99]	-16.6 [113]
+ Cutter				
▲ Changeup				
✕ Splitter				
▽ Slider	31.9%	84.4 [100]	-1.5 [85]	-30.7 [107]
◇ Curveball	15.4%	81.8 [110]	-0.7 [72]	-40.4 [115]
✦ Slow Curveball				
✱ Knuckleball				
▼ Screwball				

Arizona Diamondbacks 2020

Héctor Rondón   RHP
Born: 02/26/88   Age: 32   Bats: R   Throws: R
Height: 6'3"   Weight: 230   Origin: International Free Agent, 2004

YEAR	TEAM	LVL	AGE	W	L	SV	G	GS	IP	H	HR	BB/9	K/9	K	GB%	BABIP
2017	CHN	MLB	29	4	1	0	61	0	57^1	50	10	3.1	10.8	69	48%	.292
2018	HOU	MLB	30	2	5	15	63	0	59	58	4	3.1	10.2	67	48%	.340
2019	HOU	MLB	31	3	2	0	62	1	60^2	56	10	3.0	7.1	48	51%	.263
2020	ARI	MLB	32	2	2	0	33	0	35	32	5	3.0	8.4	33	49%	.283

Comparables: Bryan Shaw, Fernando Salas, Greg McMichael

Did you see the J.T. Realmuto eye roll gif? That's essentially what A.J. Hinch's soul was doing every time he went to put Rondón in the game in 2019. It's hard to blame him, as his double-digit K/9 rates of years past completely vanished. Oddly, his overall performance didn't suffer much, ending the season with essentially the same number of walks, runs, and innings as he did when he was the Astros closer in 2018. Maybe Hinch saw something we didn't, or maybe Rondón said something mean about pitching coach Brent Strom's shoes and never recovered. Regardless, he'll just take his fastball-slider combo to the next team that wants him and we'll be left to wonder why perfectly good relievers are so hard to appreciate.

YEAR	TEAM	LVL	AGE	WHIP	ERA	DRA	WARP	MPH	FB%	WHF	CSP
2017	CHN	MLB	29	1.22	4.24	3.29	1.2	98.6	61.6	13	47.7
2018	HOU	MLB	30	1.32	3.20	2.81	1.4	99.2	61.7	14.7	48.9
2019	HOU	MLB	31	1.25	3.71	5.72	-0.2	98.4	60.1	10.8	47.3
2020	ARI	MLB	32	1.26	4.01	4.11	0.4	97.7	60.4	12.5	47.5

Héctor Rondón, continued

Pitch Shape vs LHH

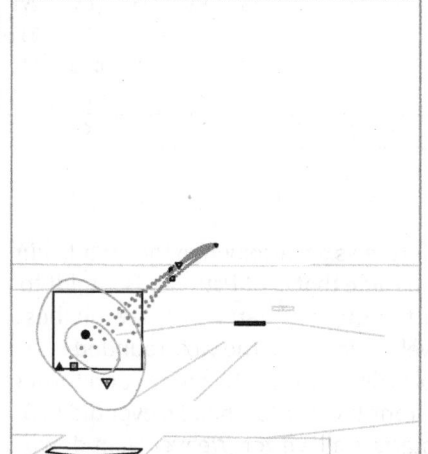

Pitch Shape vs RHH

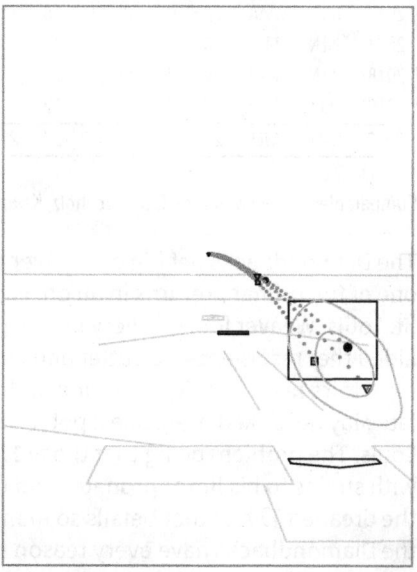

Type	Frequency	Velocity	H Movement	V Movement
● Fastball	45.9%	96.9 [113]	-6.7 [101]	-13 [108]
□ Sinker	14.2%	96.8 [122]	-14.3 [89]	-17.6 [110]
+ Cutter				
▲ Changeup	4.4%	90.8 [120]	-14.5 [85]	-25.5 [105]
✕ Splitter				
▽ Slider	35.5%	87 [111]	5.5 [102]	-33.1 [100]
◇ Curveball				
⊕ Slow Curveball				
✱ Knuckleball				
▼ Screwball				

Luke Weaver   RHP

Born: 08/21/93   Age: 26   Bats: R   Throws: R
Height: 6'2"   Weight: 170   Origin: Round 1, 2014 Draft (#27 overall)

YEAR	TEAM	LVL	AGE	W	L	SV	G	GS	IP	H	HR	BB/9	K/9	K	GB%	BABIP
2017	MEM	AAA	23	10	2	0	15	15	77^2	63	3	2.2	8.8	76	46%	.291
2017	SLN	MLB	23	7	2	0	13	10	60^1	59	7	2.5	10.7	72	51%	.335
2018	SLN	MLB	24	7	11	0	30	25	136^1	150	19	3.6	8.0	121	44%	.318
2019	ARI	MLB	25	4	3	0	12	12	64^1	55	6	2.0	9.7	69	42%	.292
2020	ARI	MLB	26	7	7	0	21	21	116	113	16	3.0	9.3	119	42%	.306

Comparables: Rafael Montero, Clay Buchholz, Kevin Gausman

The Diamondbacks bet big on Weaver's future as a starter when they made him one of the primary returns in an offseason trade that sent Paul Goldschmidt to St. Louis. Weaver looked every bit the part through 11 starts. Two new pitches aided that resurgence—a cutter and curveball gave him the well-rounded repertoire necessary for surviving multiple trips through the order—and through late May he looked more like a potential front-line starter than he ever did in St. Louis. The problem being that those 11 starts is all we got. Weaver went down with strains to his flexor pronator and UCL. After an initial scare, Weaver avoided the dreaded TJ fate that befalls so many and, with an expected return to health, the Diamondbacks have every reason to keep their chips in the middle of the table when it comes to their new emerging ace.

YEAR	TEAM	LVL	AGE	WHIP	ERA	DRA	WARP	MPH	FB%	WHF	CSP
2017	MEM	AAA	23	1.06	2.55	2.48	2.7				
2017	SLN	MLB	23	1.26	3.88	3.19	1.6	95.8	60.2	10.8	50
2018	SLN	MLB	24	1.50	4.95	4.02	1.1	96.2	57.7	10.4	40.9
2019	ARI	MLB	25	1.07	2.94	3.56	1.5	96.3	52.1	12.2	47.3
2020	ARI	MLB	26	1.31	4.15	4.32	1.9	95.8	57.5	11.2	49.4

Luke Weaver, continued

Pitch Shape vs LHH

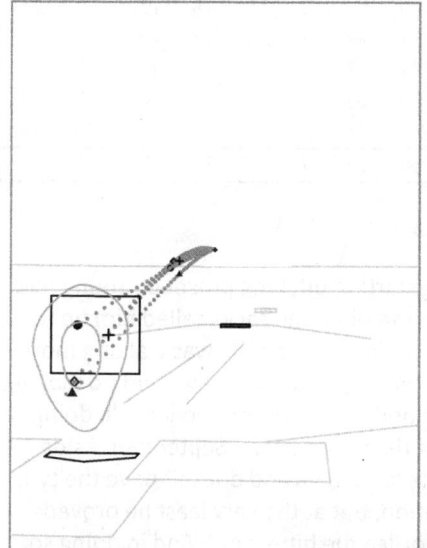

Pitch Shape vs RHH

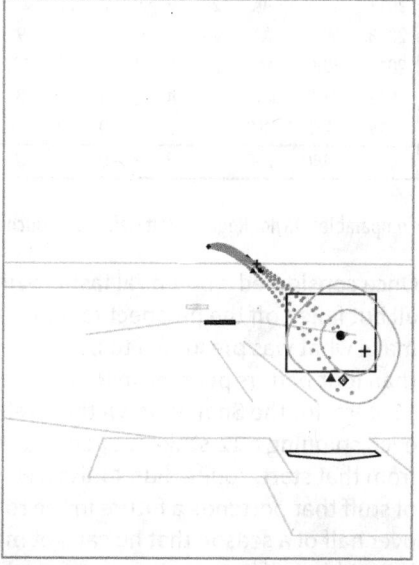

Type	Frequency	Velocity	H Movement	V Movement
● Fastball	52.1%	94.2 [105]	-7.2 [98]	-13.3 [107]
☐ Sinker				
+ Cutter	14.0%	87.8 [94]	3.4 [109]	-24.6 [98]
▲ Changeup	24.8%	84.8 [98]	-9.6 [107]	-27.8 [99]
✕ Splitter				
▽ Slider				
◇ Curveball	9.1%	81.6 [110]	1.5 [76]	-43.6 [108]
✦ Slow Curveball				
✳ Knuckleball				
▼ Screwball				

Alex Young LHP

Born: 09/09/93 Age: 26 Bats: L Throws: L
Height: 6'2" Weight: 205 Origin: Round 2, 2015 Draft (#43 overall)

YEAR	TEAM	LVL	AGE	W	L	SV	G	GS	IP	H	HR	BB/9	K/9	K	GB%	BABIP
2017	WTN	AA	23	9	9	0	27	24	137	125	12	3.8	6.8	103	47%	.275
2018	WTN	AA	24	5	1	0	9	9	50^2	49	3	2.8	8.5	48	40%	.319
2018	RNO	AAA	24	5	4	0	20	12	80	99	12	2.6	6.9	61	44%	.339
2019	RNO	AAA	25	4	3	0	20	8	54^2	66	6	4.3	10.5	64	52%	.375
2019	ARI	MLB	25	7	5	0	17	15	83^1	72	14	2.9	7.7	71	50%	.249
2020	ARI	MLB	26	3	3	0	24	8	58	55	9	3.2	8.1	52	48%	.280

Comparables: Taylor Rogers, Matt Hall, David Buchanan

Once considered a potential fast-moving starting pitching prospect, Young had all but fallen off the prospect radar when the Diamondbacks called him up to make what was presumed to be a spot start in late June. He was walking more than four batters per nine in Reno at the time, after all. Young wound up making 15 starts for the Snakes down the stretch and looked damn serviceable doing so, even spinning a 12-strikeout gem against the Reds in early September. Aside from that start, Young didn't miss a whole lot of bats and doesn't have the type of stuff that portends a future in the rotation, but at the very least he proved over half of a season that he can get major-league hitters out. And in doing so, he put himself back on the map as a multi-inning bullpen guy or rotational depth piece.

YEAR	TEAM	LVL	AGE	WHIP	ERA	DRA	WARP	MPH	FB%	WHF	CSP
2017	WTN	AA	23	1.34	3.68	5.04	0.2				
2018	WTN	AA	24	1.28	3.91	4.45	0.5				
2018	RNO	AAA	24	1.52	5.96	5.66	-0.1				
2019	RNO	AAA	25	1.68	6.09	4.35	1.1				
2019	ARI	MLB	25	1.19	3.56	4.32	1.3	90.7	36.5	13	45
2020	ARI	MLB	26	1.30	4.24	4.46	0.8	90.3	37.1	13.2	45.8

Alex Young, continued

Pitch Shape vs LHH　　　　　　**Pitch Shape vs RHH**

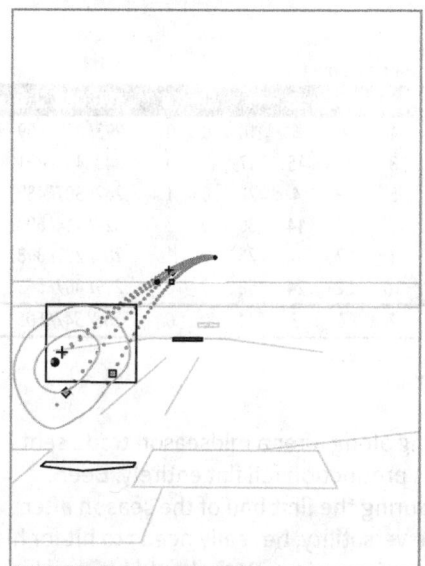 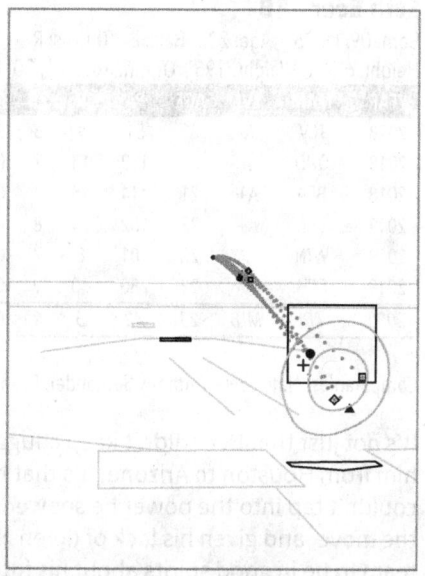

Type	Frequency	Velocity	H Movement	V Movement
● Fastball	14.5%	89.8 [93]	9 [90]	-17 [97]
□ Sinker	22.0%	89 [81]	15.5 [81]	-23.3 [90]
+ Cutter	23.0%	85 [77]	-1.1 [96]	-26.6 [91]
▲ Changeup	20.1%	84.5 [97]	13.2 [91]	-31.6 [88]
✕ Splitter				
▽ Slider				
◇ Curveball	20.5%	81.5 [109]	-1.8 [77]	-40.3 [115]
✦ Slow Curveball				
✳ Knuckleball				
▼ Screwball				

PLAYER COMMENTS WITHOUT GRAPHS

Seth Beer 1B
Born: 09/18/96 Age: 23 Bats: L Throws: R
Height: 6'3" Weight: 195 Origin: Round 1, 2018 Draft (#28 overall)

YEAR	TEAM	LVL	AGE	PA	R	2B	3B	HR	RBI	BB	K	SB	CS	AVG/OBP/SLG
2018	TCV	A-	21	51	9	3	0	4	7	6	10	0	0	.293/.431/.659
2018	QUD	A	21	132	15	7	0	3	16	15	17	1	0	.348/.443/.491
2018	BCA	A+	21	114	15	4	0	5	19	4	22	0	1	.262/.307/.439
2019	BCA	A+	22	152	24	8	0	9	34	14	30	0	3	.328/.414/.602
2019	WTN	AA	22	101	8	7	0	1	17	8	25	0	1	.205/.297/.318
2019	CCH	AA	22	280	40	9	0	16	52	24	58	0	0	.299/.407/.543
2020	ARI	MLB	23	42	6	2	0	2	7	3	11	0	0	.268/.347/.505

Comparables: Nate Lowe, Anthony Santander, Ryan O'Hearn

It's not just that Beer didn't keep chugging along after a midseason trade sent him from Houston to Arizona, it's that his production fell flat entirely. Beer couldn't tap into the power he showed during the first half of the season after the move, and given his lack of defensive versatility, he really needs to hit for his team to be in good spirits about his future. To be clear, Beer should hit, and his stout frame possesses enough power to leave scouts frothing at the mouth when he makes contact. But the bar for prospects who offer no utility elsewhere is so high that hiccups such as Beer's second half are enough to leave you feeling bitter about his future potential.

YEAR	TEAM	LVL	AGE	PA	DRC+	VORP	BABIP	BRR	FRAA	WARP
2018	TCV	A-	21	51	188	7.7	.296	-0.8	LF(7): -1.0, 1B(4): -0.1	0.3
2018	QUD	A	21	132	166	11.6	.391	-1.2	RF(10): -0.9, LF(9): -1.1	0.8
2018	BCA	A+	21	114	110	1.1	.288	-2.2	LF(13): -1.4, 1B(6): -0.2	-0.1
2019	BCA	A+	22	152	189	14.6	.359	-1.6	1B(16): 0.0, LF(15): -0.7	1.3
2019	WTN	AA	22	101	74	-0.2	.270	0.0	1B(14): -0.7, LF(9): -0.4	-0.2
2019	CCH	AA	22	280	177	21.5	.333	-3.1	1B(46): 0.8, LF(8): -0.1	2.1
2020	ARI	MLB	23	42	122	2.3	.320	-0.1	LF 0	0.2

Jake McCarthy   OF

Born: 07/30/97   Age: 22   Bats: L   Throws: L
Height: 6'2"   Weight: 195   Origin: Round 1, 2018 Draft (#39 overall)

YEAR	TEAM	LVL	AGE	PA	R	2B	3B	HR	RBI	BB	K	SB	CS	AVG/OBP/SLG
2018	YAK	A-	20	241	33	17	3	3	18	22	40	20	8	.288/.378/.442
2019	VIS	A+	21	214	29	13	3	2	30	17	52	18	2	.277/.341/.405
2020	ARI	MLB	22	251	23	13	1	5	24	15	71	9	4	.227/.283/.352

Comparables: Zoilo Almonte, Kirk Nieuwenhuis, Kyle Lewis

"The past cannot be changed. The future is in your power." That unattributed quote is doubly true for the Diamondbacks' second first-round pick in 2018 following a season mostly lost to injuries, in which he didn't show the power potential many believe he has. McCarthy has good wheels and projects to stick in center field, but a couple of injuries—including one to his ankle that shut him down for the season in July—limited him to just 53 games. In the games he did play, he handled the stick about as well as hoped, he just couldn't lift the danged ball over the fence. The injuries are troubling, especially given his aggressive play in the field, but his potential is still that of a solid regular, given some luck in the health department.

YEAR	TEAM	LVL	AGE	PA	DRC+	VORP	BABIP	BRR	FRAA	WARP
2018	YAK	A-	20	241	143	20.4	.341	-0.5	CF(44): 8.0, LF(11): -2.3	2.2
2019	VIS	A+	21	214	104	15.2	.369	5.0	CF(53): -0.6	1.2
2020	ARI	MLB	22	251	70	-0.7	.308	0.9	CF 2, LF 0	0.1

Arizona Diamondbacks 2020

Kristian Robinson OF

Born: 12/11/00 Age: 19 Bats: R Throws: R
Height: 6'3" Weight: 190 Origin: International Free Agent, 2017

YEAR	TEAM	LVL	AGE	PA	R	2B	3B	HR	RBI	BB	K	SB	CS	AVG/OBP/SLG
2018	DIA	RK	17	182	35	11	0	4	31	16	46	7	5	.272/.341/.414
2018	MSO	RK	17	74	13	1	0	3	10	11	21	5	3	.300/.419/.467
2019	YAK	A-	18	189	29	10	1	9	35	23	47	14	3	.319/.407/.558
2019	KNC	A	18	102	14	3	1	5	16	8	30	3	2	.217/.294/.435
2020	ARI	MLB	19	251	25	11	1	7	27	22	85	5	3	.227/.301/.370

Comparables: Ronald Acuña Jr., Fernando Tatis Jr., Yorman Rodriguez

In another universe, Robinson would have spent parts of 2019 touring the Northwest looking at college campuses, weighing where to continue his education, before ultimately deciding to go to Northwestern. In this universe, the 18-year-old went to many of the same places, only instead of touring campuses he was torturing opposing pitchers in the Northwest League. Speaking of another universe, Robinson seemingly defies physics; he's imposing in the box and explosive outside of it. In one reality, he ended up in Northwestern (Medicine Field); in this one, he received his first dose of higher education in full-season ball. There's a steep learning curve, but Robinson has every tool available to him to aid in his success. He ranked No. 100 on our 2019 list entering the season. Will he rank higher this year? You can check the back of the book and find out, but really, it's academic.

YEAR	TEAM	LVL	AGE	PA	DRC+	VORP	BABIP	BRR	FRAA	WARP
2018	DIA	RK	17	182	126	9.5	.351	1.3	CF(26): -5.3, LF(6): -0.9	0.7
2018	MSO	RK	17	74	119	6.0	.405	0.5	CF(10): -2.3, LF(7): 0.4	0.0
2019	YAK	A-	18	189	208	24.4	.398	-0.1	CF(21): 1.6, RF(18): 3.8	2.8
2019	KNC	A	18	102	91	3.0	.263	-0.3	CF(18): 0.6, RF(5): 0.2	0.2
2020	ARI	MLB	19	251	81	1.7	.332	-0.1	CF 1, RF 1	0.4

Pavin Smith 1B

Born: 02/06/96 Age: 24 Bats: L Throws: L
Height: 6'2" Weight: 210 Origin: Round 1, 2017 Draft (#7 overall)

YEAR	TEAM	LVL	AGE	PA	R	2B	3B	HR	RBI	BB	K	SB	CS	AVG/OBP/SLG
2017	YAK	A-	21	223	34	15	2	0	27	27	24	2	1	.318/.401/.415
2018	VIS	A+	22	504	63	25	1	11	54	57	65	3	2	.255/.343/.392
2019	WTN	AA	23	507	62	29	6	12	67	59	61	2	1	.291/.370/.466
2020	ARI	MLB	24	251	26	13	1	7	29	22	43	0	0	.249/.317/.409

Comparables: Matt Thaiss, Yonder Alonso, Alex Hassan

The flaws in Smith's profile were apparent from the moment he was drafted: He was defensively limited to first base and had a flat bat path that didn't generate a lot of power. All of that coalesced into a powerless first full season in the California League. Smith showed signs of a swing change in 2019 and combined his keen eye and bat control with a little bit of pop, finishing with the sixth-best slugging percentage in the Southern League. There's little question that Smith will hit in the majors, but the development of his power will be the difference between whether as a solid regular or someone who hits enough to keep his job but consistently leaves employers wanting.

YEAR	TEAM	LVL	AGE	PA	DRC+	VORP	BABIP	BRR	FRAA	WARP
2017	YAK	A-	21	223	162	15.3	.363	-1.8	1B(42): 1.0	1.5
2018	VIS	A+	22	504	112	9.5	.275	-1.1	1B(109): 9.0, RF(1): -0.1	2.0
2019	WTN	AA	23	507	142	25.1	.310	-5.9	1B(78): 2.5, RF(28): -2.6	2.5
2020	ARI	MLB	24	251	92	5.3	.278	-0.4	1B 2, RF 0	0.8

Arizona Diamondbacks 2020

Alek Thomas   OF

Born: 04/28/00   Age: 20   Bats: L   Throws: L
Height: 5'11"   Weight: 175   Origin: Round 2, 2018 Draft (#63 overall)

YEAR	TEAM	LVL	AGE	PA	R	2B	3B	HR	RBI	BB	K	SB	CS	AVG/OBP/SLG
2018	DIA	RK	18	138	24	3	5	0	10	13	18	8	2	.325/.394/.431
2018	MSO	RK	18	134	26	11	1	2	17	11	19	4	3	.341/.396/.496
2019	KNC	A	19	402	63	21	7	8	48	43	72	11	6	.312/.393/.479
2019	VIS	A+	19	104	13	2	0	2	7	9	33	4	5	.255/.327/.340
2020	ARI	MLB	20	251	25	12	2	6	27	20	64	3	1	.256/.320/.393

Comparables: Victor Robles, Billy McKinney, Byron Buxton

You go to the hardware store and see a display for a beautiful new barbecue pit. You picture that pit in your backyard and know it's gonna be the best Summer ever. Hosting get-togethers for birthdays, anniversaries, or just because the weather's nice. The sun is shining, a cool breeze is blowing, and the cooler is filled with ice cold beer. You buy it and bring the box home, only to find complicated instructions on how to build the pit. This is the moment of truth. To realize your dream, you've got to follow the instructions perfectly. One misstep—a screw too loose or slotting Part J into Part Q instead of Part R—and your perfect barbecue-filled Summer will come crashing down. Thomas has everything you want in an above-average major league outfielder—a smooth swing, good speed, an athletic frame, and a good feel for the strike zone. But Thomas is still in the box. He aced his first look at full-season ball, torching Low-A and holding his own upon promotion. There's plenty there to envision a top-of-the-order hitter, it just all needs to be put together correctly. Any variance and the barbecue pit falls apart and that starter becomes a fourth outfielder, and you find yourself glancing over at your neighbor's young outfielder saying "why doesn't mine look like that?"

YEAR	TEAM	LVL	AGE	PA	DRC+	VORP	BABIP	BRR	FRAA	WARP
2018	DIA	RK	18	138	162	15.2	.381	1.6	CF(13): -2.1, LF(11): -2.4	0.8
2018	MSO	RK	18	134	160	7.9	.392	-1.0	CF(21): 0.1, LF(7): 0.5	0.8
2019	KNC	A	19	402	153	32.4	.372	0.4	CF(75): -10.1, RF(7): 0.8	2.5
2019	VIS	A+	19	104	90	3.7	.373	0.4	CF(23): 2.6	0.6
2020	ARI	MLB	20	251	90	4.8	.332	-0.2	CF -2, LF 0	0.3

Yasmany Tomás   OF/1B

Born: 11/14/90   Age: 29   Bats: R   Throws: R
Height: 6'2"   Weight: 250   Origin: International Free Agent, 2014

YEAR	TEAM	LVL	AGE	PA	R	2B	3B	HR	RBI	BB	K	SB	CS	AVG/OBP/SLG
2017	ARI	MLB	26	180	19	11	1	8	32	13	50	0	0	.241/.294/.464
2018	RNO	AAA	27	371	42	22	4	14	65	11	101	2	0	.262/.280/.465
2019	RNO	AAA	28	431	63	24	3	29	82	22	110	2	0	.301/.341/.590
2019	ARI	MLB	28	6	0	0	0	0	0	0	3	0	0	.000/.000/.000
2020	ARI	MLB	29	251	29	11	1	12	35	12	76	1	1	.243/.281/.451

Comparables: Hunter Pence, Avisaíl García, Laynce Nix

In the fifth year of an ill-fated six-year contract, Tomás accomplished something he failed to do a year prior: He made it back to the majors, albeit for four games and six hitless plate appearances. Tomás also mashed in the hitter-friendly Pacific Coast League, something he likewise failed to do in the past, though credit can likely be shared with a livelier baseball. It's anyone but Tomás' fault that the previous Arizona regime guaranteed him $68.5 million all those years ago, and the 29-year-old will most likely play out the final year of the contract in Reno once more, working to hit his way back to Arizona while raking in a cool $17 million.

YEAR	TEAM	LVL	AGE	PA	DRC+	VORP	BABIP	BRR	FRAA	WARP
2017	ARI	MLB	26	180	82	5.7	.294	-0.3	LF(42): -7.1	-0.7
2018	RNO	AAA	27	371	72	-3.3	.322	-3.4	LF(44): -5.9, 1B(9): -0.3	-1.4
2019	RNO	AAA	28	431	98	6.9	.348	-2.6	1B(46): 2.3, LF(44): -2.8	0.5
2019	ARI	MLB	28	6	78	0.0	.000	0.0		0.0
2020	ARI	MLB	29	251	88	3.8	.304	-0.2	LF -5, 1B 0	-0.1

Daulton Varsho C

Born: 07/02/96 Age: 23 Bats: L Throws: R
Height: 5'10" Weight: 190 Origin: Round 2, 2017 Draft (#68 overall)

YEAR	TEAM	LVL	AGE	PA	R	2B	3B	HR	RBI	BB	K	SB	CS	AVG/OBP/SLG
2017	YAK	A-	20	212	36	16	3	7	39	17	30	7	2	.311/.368/.534
2018	VIS	A+	21	342	44	11	3	11	44	30	71	19	3	.286/.363/.451
2019	WTN	AA	22	452	85	25	4	18	58	42	63	21	5	.301/.378/.520
2020	ARI	MLB	23	70	9	4	1	3	10	5	15	1	0	.271/.332/.498

Comparables: Max Stassi, Kyle Lewis, Nate Lowe

YEAR	TEAM	P. COUNT	FRM RUNS	BLK RUNS	THRW RUNS	TOT RUNS
2019	WTN	10022	-4.0	0.0	-3.5	-7.1
2020	ARI	1280	-0.6	-0.1	-0.2	-0.9

Teams are finding it increasingly tough to develop catchers who provide value on both sides of the ball. Like so many other young catchers, Varsho has one side of that proposition covered, having battered the Southern League in his first look at Double-A pitching. The question, though, resides with his defense, and if it takes a little longer than expected for him to reach the majors, that'll be the reason. Catcher development is weird, though, so when Varsho turns out to be a Gold Glove backstop with a fringy bat, don't blame us.

YEAR	TEAM	LVL	AGE	PA	DRC+	VORP	BABIP	BRR	FRAA	WARP
2017	YAK	A-	20	212	156	24.2	.338	2.4	C(36): 0.8	2.3
2018	VIS	A+	21	342	131	30.5	.341	2.5	C(55): 1.4	2.7
2019	WTN	AA	22	452	156	52.6	.317	5.9	C(75): -5.7, CF(4): -1.2	4.3
2020	ARI	MLB	23	70	112	4.3	.304	0.2	C -1, CF 0	0.3

J.B. Bukauskas RHP

Born: 10/11/96   Age: 23   Bats: R   Throws: R
Height: 6'0"   Weight: 196   Origin: Round 1, 2017 Draft (#15 overall)

YEAR	TEAM	LVL	AGE	W	L	SV	G	GS	IP	H	HR	BB/9	K/9	K	GB%	BABIP
2017	TCV	A-	20	0	0	0	2	2	6	4	0	6.0	9.0	6	53%	.267
2018	TCV	A-	21	0	0	0	3	3	8^1	8	0	2.2	9.7	9	46%	.364
2018	QUD	A	21	1	2	0	4	4	15	15	0	4.2	12.6	21	55%	.395
2018	BCA	A+	21	3	0	0	5	5	28	13	1	4.2	10.0	31	59%	.194
2018	CCH	AA	21	0	0	0	1	1	6	1	0	3.0	12.0	8	60%	.100
2019	CCH	AA	22	2	4	1	20	14	85^2	81	8	5.7	10.3	98	48%	.332
2019	WTN	AA	22	0	1	0	2	2	7	10	0	6.4	14.1	11	39%	.556
2020	ARI	MLB	23	1	1	0	11	0	11	11	2	3.7	8.8	11	44%	.299

Comparables: Logan Webb, Jorge Alcala, Nick Tropeano

One year after reportedly being included in a trade proposal that would've sent Bryce Harper to the Houston Astros, Bukauskas was instead shipped to Arizona in the Zack Greinke swap. Bukauskas has perhaps the highest ceiling of any of the players the Diamondbacks acquired for their erstwhile ace, but counters that ceiling with significant bullpen risk. His fastball sits 92-94 and he can get it into the mid-90s when he really amps it up. He has a nasty, wipeout slider with depth, and a cutter and changeup that could yet develop into above-average offerings. Far too often he isn't sure where any of those pitches are going, as evidenced by a walk rate that sat above six. Arizona bet a lot on Bukauskas, so they'll likely give him every opportunity to fail as a starter before going down the relief route.

YEAR	TEAM	LVL	AGE	WHIP	ERA	DRA	WARP	MPH	FB%	WHF	CSP
2017	TCV	A-	20	1.33	4.50	5.10	0.0				
2018	TCV	A-	21	1.20	0.00	4.27	0.1				
2018	QUD	A	21	1.47	4.20	3.95	0.2				
2018	BCA	A+	21	0.93	1.61	2.72	0.9				
2018	CCH	AA	21	0.50	0.00	2.56	0.2				
2019	CCH	AA	22	1.58	5.25	6.11	-1.3				
2019	WTN	AA	22	2.14	7.71	7.33	-0.2				
2020	ARI	MLB	23	1.38	4.34	4.50	0.1				

Arizona Diamondbacks 2020

Bo Takahashi   RHP
Born: 01/23/97   Age: 23   Bats: R   Throws: R
Height: 6'0"   Weight: 197   Origin: International Free Agent, 2014

YEAR	TEAM	LVL	AGE	W	L	SV	G	GS	IP	H	HR	BB/9	K/9	K	GB%	BABIP
2017	KNC	A	20	0	2	0	4	4	16^1	16	3	2.8	7.7	14	42%	.260
2017	VIS	A+	20	7	10	0	20	20	109^2	107	13	3.0	7.6	93	37%	.294
2018	VIS	A+	21	3	3	0	9	9	47^2	45	4	1.9	10.0	53	44%	.331
2018	WTN	AA	21	3	3	0	14	14	73	65	12	2.5	9.5	77	35%	.286
2019	WTN	AA	22	9	7	0	23	23	118^2	108	12	2.9	7.9	104	42%	.294
2020	ARI	MLB	23	1	1	0	11	0	11	12	2	3.7	7.4	9	39%	.291

Comparables: Jonathan Hernández, Sean Reid-Foley, Robert Gsellman

Throughout the course of major-league history, there have been countless players who have toiled away in the minor leagues waiting for a shot that never came. "It was like coming this close to your dreams...and then watching them brush past," said Burt Lancaster as Moonlight Graham in "Field of Dreams." Takahashi spent 5 1/2 years in the Diamondbacks' organization after signing as an international free agent as a 17-year-old in 2013. On August 18 he was called up from Double-A only to be sent back down two days later without making an appearance. The Brazilian has never much registered on the prospect radar, but has been a solid organizational soldier, one who managed a fine season in Double-A. Here's to his next major-league opportunity.

YEAR	TEAM	LVL	AGE	WHIP	ERA	DRA	WARP	MPH	FB%	WHF	CSP
2017	KNC	A	20	1.29	3.86	4.45	0.2				
2017	VIS	A+	20	1.31	5.33	4.63	0.8				
2018	VIS	A+	21	1.15	3.02	4.28	0.6				
2018	WTN	AA	21	1.16	4.68	4.30	0.9				
2019	WTN	AA	22	1.23	3.72	5.07	-0.2				
2020	ARI	MLB	23	1.45	5.20	5.32	0.0				

Taylor Widener RHP

Born: 10/24/94   Age: 25   Bats: L   Throws: R
Height: 6'0"   Weight: 195   Origin: Round 12, 2016 Draft (#368 overall)

YEAR	TEAM	LVL	AGE	W	L	SV	G	GS	IP	H	HR	BB/9	K/9	K	GB%	BABIP
2017	TAM	A+	22	7	8	0	27	27	119^1	87	5	3.8	9.7	129	45%	.273
2018	WTN	AA	23	5	8	0	26	25	137^1	99	12	2.8	11.5	176	37%	.275
2019	RNO	AAA	24	6	7	0	23	23	100	133	23	3.7	9.8	109	32%	.381
2020	ARI	MLB	25	1	1	0	11	0	11	11	2	3.6	8.8	11	34%	.305

Comparables: Jake Arrieta, Dean Deetz, Tyler Thornburg

Pitching is hard. Pitching with a rabbit/juiced/rocket ball is harder. Pitching in the notoriously hitter-friendly PCL with a juiced baseball? Good freaking luck. Widener, 2018's big riser, is still very much a pitching prospect, but his Triple-A ERA looks like a Central Michigan area code. It looked like Widener was destined for a mid-season call-up to the big club when the year began, but an early-season swoon put that thought to rest quickly. He rebounded to put together a solid second half, but the initial carnage left an unsightly final line in its wake. Consider it a setback, but not one so harmful as to keep him out of the Diamondbacks' future plans.

YEAR	TEAM	LVL	AGE	WHIP	ERA	DRA	WARP	MPH	FB%	WHF	CSP
2017	TAM	A+	22	1.15	3.39	3.05	3.1				
2018	WTN	AA	23	1.03	2.75	3.01	3.7				
2019	RNO	AAA	24	1.74	8.10	6.72	0.0				
2020	ARI	MLB	25	1.42	4.77	4.84	0.1				

Arizona Diamondbacks 2020

LINEOUTS

Hitters

HITTER	POS	TEAM	LVL	AGE	PA	R	2B	3B	HR	RBI	BB	K	SB	CS	AVG/OBP/SLG	DRC+	WARP
Blaze Alexander	SS	KNC	A	20	406	56	12	4	7	47	42	89	14	4	.262/.355/.382	120	2.5
Abraham Almonte	CF	ARI	MLB	30	38	11	3	1	1	4	7	8	0	0	.290/.421/.548	94	0.3
	CF	RNO	AAA	30	382	78	33	4	17	59	60	70	12	3	.270/.382/.558	120	1.8
Jorge Barrosa	OF	YAK	A-	18	252	25	12	2	1	26	21	32	8	4	.251/.335/.336	95	0.7
Corbin Carroll	OF	YAK	A-	18	49	13	3	4	0	6	5	12	2	0	.326/.408/.581	116	0.3
	OF	DIA	Rk	18	137	23	6	3	2	14	24	29	16	1	.288/.409/.450	161	1.3
Kevin Cron	1B	ARI	MLB	26	78	12	4	0	6	16	4	28	0	1	.211/.269/.521	83	0.0
	1B	RNO	AAA	26	377	81	20	1	38	105	61	77	1	2	.331/.449/.777	178	4.5
Tristin English	1B	YAK	A-	22	216	32	12	2	7	30	13	24	1	0	.290/.356/.482	139	1.1
Jeferson Espinal	CF	DIA	Rk	17	43	6	1	0	0	7	8	11	4	1	.286/.419/.314	127	0.4
Dominic Fletcher	OF	KNC	A	21	239	33	14	1	5	28	22	50	1	1	.318/.389/.463	145	2.2
Glenallen Hill	SS	DIA	Rk	18	181	22	4	6	3	18	17	63	19	5	.206/.289/.363	53	-0.1
Caleb Joseph	C	ARI	MLB	33	41	5	2	0	0	3	1	10	0	0	.211/.250/.263	72	0.1
	C	RNO	AAA	33	179	29	12	1	7	26	13	44	0	0	.265/.324/.481	74	0.0
Domingo Leyba	2B	RNO	AAA	23	498	85	37	3	19	77	32	78	0	2	.300/.351/.519	92	1.7
	2B	ARI	MLB	23	30	6	2	1	0	5	4	9	0	0	.280/.367/.440	84	0.1
Wyatt Mathisen	3B	DIA	Rk	25	31	4	3	0	0	3	6	3	1	0	.348/.516/.478	201	0.4
	3B	RNO	AAA	25	345	72	19	1	23	61	39	84	1	0	.283/.403/.601	122	2.2
Wilderd Patino	OF	MSO	Rk+	17	40	6	1	2	0	4	2	14	1	1	.229/.300/.371	43	-0.1
	OF	DIA	Rk	17	125	18	4	3	1	21	11	32	13	3	.349/.403/.472	147	1.1
Andy Yerzy	1B	YAK	A-	20	272	30	11	0	6	34	37	61	1	1	.220/.331/.345	92	-0.1
	1B	KNC	A	20	136	8	5	0	0	5	9	39	0	0	.104/.176/.144	5	-1.2
Andy Young	INF	WTN	AA	25	263	36	15	2	8	28	18	53	1	1	.260/.363/.453	128	1.2
	INF	RNO	AAA	25	277	53	10	3	21	53	24	68	2	2	.280/.373/.611	110	1.5

Blaze Alexander is fast (yes, really), touts a big arm and has a solid glove that should stick at short. How his bat progresses as he moves up the ladder will be the key to the former 11th-round pick going from being an intriguing prospect to a legitimate one. ⚾ **Abraham Almonte**'s nickname is, according to Baseball Reference, "El Varon," which translates to The Man. After playing for five teams in seven major league seasons, he should consider becoming "The Emergency Plan." ⚾ **Jorge Barrosa** held his own in Low-A and has the defensive prowess and on-base skill to project as solid regular down the road. ⚾ **Corbin Carroll** was one of the better prep bats in this year's draft and hit the snot out of the ball in his professional debut. He has a pure and advanced stroke and can take the ball to all fields, and has the tools to stick in center. ⚾ **Kevin Cron** got his first taste of big-league action and promptly struck out in nearly half of his plate appearances. At age 26, he's likely to shed the "C.J.'s brother" label, which is considerably less impressive than, say, being Corey Seager's brother. ⚾ A third-round pick out of the Georgia Institute of Technology, **Tristin English** didn't put any particular spin on his professional debut. He straight waxed the Northwest League. ⓧ Precocious slash-and-burn outfield prospect **Jeferson Espinal** arrived stateside just two months after his 17th birthday, where he showed enough tools to receive the prized "helium prospect" tag. ⓧ **Dominic Fletcher** does virtually everything well but has no real standout tool. The fourth-round pick out of Arkansas and brother of David can play all three outfield positions. He projects as a likely fourth outfielder at the next level. ⓧ The Diamondbacks inked **Alvin Guzmán** to a $1.85M deal during the 2018 international signing period. He's yet to play stateside, but is pretty much your prototypical raw, toolsy, J2 outfielder who is two years away from being two years away. ⓧ The Diamondbacks selected **Glenallen Hill Jr.** in the fourth round of the 2019 draft, and the 19-year-old shortstop shares his father's name, but at 5-foot-9, 160 pounds, literally nothing else. ⓧ **Caleb Joseph** has hung around the bigs thanks to his sterling reputation as a defender behind the plate, but even that can't salvage an increasingly bleak batting line. ⓧ The shine has faded a bit on **Domingo Leyba**'s star after injuries plagued the former top prospect, but he acquitted himself well in a cup of coffee at the majors and could stick as a backup infielder. ⓧ He might have spent the last year in Reno kicking all around the dirt and knocking guys around, but **Wyatt Mathisen** is less a old west gunslinger (despite his name) and more an up-and-down guy who benefitted from a crazy offensive environment. ⓧ Stop if you've heard this one before: **Wilderd Patino** is a tooled up, up-the-middle prospect who was born after the turn of the century and could be the Next Big Prospect. ⓧ Something weird happened on **Andy Yerzy**'s way toward becoming one of those bat-first catching prospects with questions about whether he'd stick behind the plate: He stopped hitting. ⓧ The quaternary piece of the Diamondbacks' return for Paul Goldschmidt, **Andy Young** acquitted himself well at the upper levels of the minors. He plays all over the dirt and as a 37th-round pick a brief summation of his scouting report must have read something like "Young, Andy: Restless."

Arizona Diamondbacks 2020

Pitchers

PITCHER	TEAM	LVL	AGE	W	L	SV	G	GS	IP	H	HR	BB/9	K/9	K	GB%	WHIP	ERA	DRA	WARP
Taylor Clarke	VIS	A+	26	1	0	0	1	1	6	3	0	0.0	4.5	3	71%	0.50	0.00	2.88	0.2
	RNO	AAA	26	3	1	0	8	8	36^2	41	6	4.2	6.9	28	36%	1.58	6.63	4.95	0.6
	ARI	MLB	26	5	5	1	23	15	84^2	86	23	3.2	7.2	68	40%	1.37	5.31	6.46	-0.7
Stefan Crichton	RNO	AAA	27	4	3	1	36	0	57^1	52	4	2.4	8.2	52	58%	1.17	3.61	2.45	2.1
	ARI	MLB	27	1	0	0	28	0	30^1	23	3	2.4	9.8	33	52%	1.02	3.56	3.72	0.5
Luis Frias	YAK	A-	21	3	3	0	10	10	49^2	36	0	3.1	13.0	72	42%	1.07	1.99	3.56	0.9
	KNC	A	21	3	1	0	6	6	26^2	22	1	4.1	9.8	29	37%	1.27	4.39	4.78	0.1
Josh Green	VIS	A+	23	9	1	0	14	14	78	69	1	1.5	8.0	69	67%	1.05	1.73	3.94	1.0
	WTN	AA	23	2	4	0	8	8	48^1	61	2	1.5	6.0	32	67%	1.43	4.28	6.09	-0.7
Greg Holland	HAR	AA	33	1	0	0	8	0	9	4	0	3.0	9.0	9	41%	0.78	0.00	3.44	0.1
	ARI	MLB	33	1	2	17	40	0	35^2	25	5	6.1	10.3	41	45%	1.37	4.54	4.46	0.3
Drey Jameson	YAK	A-	21	0	0	0	8	8	11^2	14	1	6.9	9.3	12	42%	1.97	6.17	7.64	-0.3
Levi Kelly	KNC	A	20	5	1	0	22	22	100^1	72	4	3.5	11.3	126	48%	1.11	2.15	3.17	2.4
Matthew Koch	RNO	AAA	28	5	10	0	21	17	100	135	21	2.7	7.3	81	42%	1.65	7.38	5.55	1.1
	ARI	MLB	28	0	0	0	9	0	20^2	29	8	1.7	3.9	9	36%	1.60	9.15	8.69	-0.7
Yoan Lopez	ARI	MLB	26	2	7	1	70	0	60^2	52	11	2.5	6.2	42	44%	1.14	3.41	5.17	0.1
Brennan Malone	DIA	Rk	18	1	2	0	6	3	7	4	0	6.4	9.0	7	29%	1.29	5.14	3.32	0.2
Ryne Nelson	YAK	A-	21	0	1	0	10	7	18^2	15	1	4.8	12.5	26	46%	1.34	2.89	4.32	0.2
Joel Payamps	WTN	AA	25	3	4	0	7	7	40^2	40	2	0.4	8.6	39	49%	1.03	2.88	3.76	0.6
	RNO	AAA	25	2	2	0	8	8	38	41	6	3.8	7.1	30	43%	1.50	4.97	4.45	0.8
	ARI	MLB	25	0	0	0	2	0	4	4	0	6.8	6.8	3	18%	1.75	4.50	5.68	0.0
Robby Scott	RNO	AAA	29	3	0	1	41	0	48	42	10	6.6	11.4	61	30%	1.60	6.94	4.39	0.9
	ARI	MLB	29	1	0	0	11	0	7^1	8	1	8.6	11.0	9	33%	2.05	4.91	4.86	0.0
Jimmie Sherfy	RNO	AAA	27	2	3	12	35	0	35	32	2	5.4	12.6	49	41%	1.51	3.60	3.22	1.0
	ARI	MLB	27	1	0	1	17	0	18^1	23	4	2.5	10.8	22	22%	1.53	5.89	5.90	-0.1
Riley Smith	WTN	AA	24	4	4	0	13	13	71^1	65	4	2.0	7.8	62	51%	1.14	2.27	3.90	0.9
	RNO	AAA	24	2	2	0	12	12	62^2	85	15	2.9	6.9	48	44%	1.68	6.89	6.89	-0.1
Matt Tabor	KNC	A	20	5	4	0	21	21	95^1	79	6	1.5	9.5	101	44%	1.00	2.93	3.30	2.1
Emilio Vargas	DIA	Rk	22	0	2	0	3	3	10^1	9	1	1.7	10.5	12	36%	1.06	4.35	2.36	0.4
	WTN	AA	22	5	3	0	17	17	85^2	74	10	2.4	7.4	70	44%	1.13	3.78	4.52	0.5
Blake Walston	YAK	A-	18	0	0	0	3	3	6	6	0	3.0	9.0	6	41%	1.33	3.00	5.95	-0.1

Silvino Bracho avoided yet another season of riding the bus between Phoenix and Reno, but unfortunately it was because Tommy John surgery cost him all of it. ⊗ **Taylor Clarke** is pretty much the epitome of a sixth starter, and given his nondescript name and role you'd be forgiven for forgetting he exists. If you did, though, you'd also be forgetting his wife, whose name is Taylor Clarke. ⊗ **Stefan Crichton** was called up to Arizona six different times during the season and until rosters expanded in September, never spent more than eight consecutive days there. ⓑ **Luis Frias** burst onto the scene with a dominating performance in the Northwest League and looks the part of a future starter if he can develop another offering to go with his plus-fastball and plus-curve. ⓑ Arizona transitioned **Josh Green** from a reliever to a starter this year and he promptly dominated High-A and held his own in a late-season audition at Double-A. The former 14th-round pick doesn't miss a ton of bats, but his sinking fastball induces a lot of grounders. ⓑ **Tommy Henry** grew up in Michigan and, unlike Derek Jeter, honored his commitment to play collegiately at the University of Michigan. He has an 80-grade pitch face and the type of stuff that will likely confine him to a bullpen role long term. ⓑ Baseball Reference shows **Greg Holland**'s nickname as "The Dirty South." He earned the moniker last season as his 16 percent walk rate meant there were few clean innings, and as a result, his numbers went south. ⓑ **Drey Jameson** was taken as a comp pick first-rounder and signed under-slot after some reported issues with his physical. He's an undersized right-hander with a busy delivery who has a lot to overcome to stick as a starter. ⓑ **Levi Kelly** took a step forward by missing a whole lotta bats in the Midwest League. He has three potential above-average offerings but might end up in the bullpen. ⓑ **Matt Koch's** surname is pronounced "cook," as in the present verb form of "cooked"—or, the answer to the question: "how'd Koch look today?" ⓑ Making the majors meant **Yoan López** could finally transition from the "Dave Stewart gave this dude $8.25 million?!" phase of his career to the "fairly anonymous middle reliever" phase. At least he throws real hard. ⓑ **Brennan Malone** has the look, velocity, and wipeout breaker of a future starter. There's a ton of development and projection left for the first-rounder. ⓑ **Ryne Nelson** was taken in the second round out of Oregon and looks like the second coming of Tyler Clippard, both in terms of his delivery and his specs. ⓑ **Joel Payamps** was added to the Diamondbacks' 40-man roster last offseason and seemed a good candidate to factor into their bullpen plans, but a broken foot limited him to just 17 appearances total between the minors and majors. ⓑ **Robby Scott** went from major-league caliber arm dominating Triple-A for a World Series champion to someone who not only couldn't crack the bullpen in Arizona, but couldn't find the plate in Reno, either. ⓑ **Jimmie Sherfy** has never been able to harness his funky delivery enough to deliver consistent results. Plus, his name sounds like a clothing brand for surfers. ⓑ LSU draftees finished second and fourth in AL MVP voting in 2019. No pressure, **Riley Smith**. Then again, as a 24th-round pick, just making the majors might be a comparable achievement for the right-hander. ⓑ **Matt Tabor** throws strikes, which is important because none of his offerings are considered above-average. ⓑ **Emilio Vargas** emerged as a viable starting pitching prospect in 2018 and picked up where he left off in his second go at Double-A. He has an electric fastball and could work his way into a rotation if he continues to develop his secondaries. ⑬ **Blake Walston** is a tall lefty with a clean arm action and the type of athleticism you expect from a former quarterback and first-round pick.

Diamondbacks Prospects

The State of the System
Seven draft picks in the first 75 will improve your system health quite quickly. A few breakout teenaged IFAs don't hurt either, and the Diamondbacks now have one of the deeper systems in baseball.

The Top Ten

1
★ ★ ★ *2020 Top 101 Prospect* **#16** ★ ★ ★

Kristian Robinson   OF   OFP: 70   ETA: Late 2022
Born: 12/11/00   Age: 19   Bats: R   Throws: R   Height: 6'3"   Weight: 190
Origin: International Free Agent, 2017

The Report: Robinson is an intimidating presence. His extra-large frame and long, strong legs make for a dynamic athlete. And at just 19, he already has great body control for his size. During batting practice Robinson shows off prodigious power to all fields. He can consistently get the ball in the air, and although in-game power is a work in progress due to his still-developing hit tool, he hit some mammoth shots with Kane County. Robinson is a patient hitter, rarely swinging at first pitches, but at this stage he does tend to expand the zone quite a bit with two strikes, and has also struggled against breakers. His swing is loose, highlighting a lightning-quick bat that stays through the zone a long time. Robinson has solid balance and rhythm in the box, and he uses his lower half well.

On the basepaths, he runs like a deer. His long strides, paired with improving agility, will lead to stolen bases once he understands how to swipe a bag. Patrolling the outfield Robinson flashes the ability to be a plus center fielder, making numerous impressive catches. He still needs to refine his jumps and route efficiency, but when he learns the position better he should have no problem contending for Gold Gloves. His arm already sits plus. Even when on the move he is able to get his lower half engaged and throw a strike to any base. Once Robinson improves his instincts with reps he has the potential to be a true five-tool outfielder with a long and successful big-league career.

Variance: High. Robinson is very young and still needs to develop quite a bit, especially his hit tool in order to max-out his power game.

Mark Barry's Fantasy Take: Athletic. Potential five-tool stud. Upside. Bahamas. And that, my friends, is Kristian Robinson bingo. To be fair, though, it's hard to discuss Robinson without most, if not all of these descriptors, as the 18-year-old hit 14 homers and stole 17 bags in just under 300 trips to the plate. There are plenty of swings and misses in his game, but if everything clicks, hooooo boy. Robinson is a pretty clear top-25 dynasty guy right now.

--- ★ ★ ★ *2020 Top 101 Prospect* **#54** ★ ★ ★ ---

2. Alek Thomas OF — OFP: 60 ETA: 2022
Born: 04/28/00 Age: 20 Bats: L Throws: L Height: 5'11" Weight: 175
Origin: Round 2, 2018 Draft (#63 overall)

The Report: Thomas might end up being the best pure hitter from the 2018 draft class. As a teenager he excelled in the Midwest League, earning a place on the Futures Game roster and a late season promotion to High-A. Offensively, his sweet, left-handed swing is quick and compact and he shows a disciplined approach. The bat speed and strength provide some sneaky pop, but it's presently geared mostly for gap-to-gap, line-drive power. After contact, he accelerates quickly out of the box and has plus raw speed. It's the type of acceleration that allows for extra bases and eventually, as he becomes more experienced, the occasional stolen base. Defensively, his quick-twitch athleticism allows him to cover plenty of ground in center field. That plus range and solid instincts make for a future above-average outfielder.

Variance: High. Thomas' athleticism and defensive ability give a fairly high floor but he's still a teenager who has yet to face advanced pitching.

Mark Barry's Fantasy Take: Thomas is a plus runner who hits tons of line drives with gap power which makes him extremely #myjam. He doesn't need to hit a ton of homers to be useful in fantasy circles, but if the ball stays juiced, Thomas is a guy who could certainly benefit. He doesn't quite have Robinson's ceiling, but he's still a top-40ish dynasty prospect.

--- ★ ★ ★ *2020 Top 101 Prospect* **#87** ★ ★ ★ ---

3. Daulton Varsho C — OFP: 55 ETA: Early 2021
Born: 07/02/96 Age: 23 Bats: L Throws: R Height: 5'10" Weight: 190
Origin: Round 2, 2017 Draft (#68 overall)

The Report: Varsho's bat took another step forward in the Southern League in 2019. He got less pull-happy, improving both his approach and contact rate, while putting more balls over the fence due to his strong, fireplug frame. Both the hit and power tools here are potentially above-average.

Varsho is deceptively quick and athletic and that helps him both on the basepaths and behind the plate, although his receiving remains a work in progress. He has a plus, accurate arm, and he's improved year-over-year defensively as a pro. The bat is likely to be major-league-ready well before the glove though.

Variance: High. So the offensive variance here is, at worst, medium. We think Varsho will be an above-average hitter in the majors, which gets him well over the bar for catcher offense. Catcher defense is trickier though, and he's never caught more than 76 games in a season. He has the frame for it, but the defensive chops aren't there yet, and that could make the ultimate projection trickier. If he even gets to average defensively though, the bat could make him an occasional All-Star behind the dish.

Mark Barry's Fantasy Take: If you're going to trust a catching prospect (and generally, you probably should not) Varsho isn't a bad one to roll with, offering a potent power/speed combo rarely seen behind the dish. He's not a great defender though, so he'll need to continue progressing with the glove to keep that sweet, sweet catcher eligibility. He has the offensive chops to be a top-five backstop, if he sticks, though.

─── ★ ★ ★ *2020 Top 101 Prospect* **#91** ★ ★ ★ ───

4 Geraldo Perdomo SS   OFP: 55   ETA: 2021
Born: 10/22/99   Age: 20   Bats: B   Throws: R   Height: 6'3"   Weight: 184
Origin: International Free Agent, 2016

The Report: The 19-year-old shortstop slashed .275/.397/364 with 21 doubles and 26 steals while playing 116 games at two different levels of A-ball in the 2019 season. The switch-hitting Perdomo stays inside the baseball exceptionally well, and utilizes a high rate of contact to generate line drives gap-to-gap. He's displayed more power from the left side of the plate in the minors, hitting all eight of his career home runs against right-handed pitching. He shows advanced strike-zone awareness (169 BB/148 K in 1034 PAs as pro) and a proclivity to lay down bunts, further showcasing his adept control of the box and the bat.

The plus runner utilizes long strides to gather ground between bases, and on defense where he's demonstrated good range and mobility at shortstop. His exceptional hand-eye coordination and receptive hands eat up grounders and pair with a solid throwing arm, allowing him to make most plays at shortstop. His athleticism and advanced baseball acumen would enable him to succeed at any defensive position in the infield or outfield, perhaps making him most valuable as a super-utility player. Perdomo's advanced offensive game, defensive versatility, and baseball instincts allow him to impact a game in a multitude of ways. He should be on the fast-track to Arizona.

Variance: Medium. Perdomo's still in A-ball, but his advanced offensive game and baseball savvy increase his value and set a high-floor.

Arizona Diamondbacks 2020

Mark Barry's Fantasy Take: In the Midseason Top 50, Bret tabbed Perdomo as having Elvis Andrus + Walks upside. Bret is the boss, so I won't argue with him. I like Perdomo quite a bit.

5 | Corbin Carroll   OF   OFP: 55   ETA: 2023
Born: 08/21/00   Age: 19   Bats: L   Throws: L   Height: 5'10"   Weight: 165
Origin: Round 1, 2019 Draft (#16 overall)

The Report: Despite being an undersized prep outfielder, and a bit of a throwback profile, Carroll had first-round buzz all spring, and didn't make it past the first of the Diamondbacks' plethora of picks. For the 16th-overall pick Arizona got a quick-twitch, up-the-middle defender, with good wrists and above-average bat speed. Carroll has a flat swing plane, generating line drives and ground balls. He's strong enough to put some sting into them, though, and his high-end plus speed will rack up both infield hits and extra bases in the gaps. Carroll should stick in center field and has an above-average arm. The lack of power might ultimately limit the upside here, but it's an intriguing package overall as a hit-and-speed top of the order bat that can go get it at a premium defensive position.

Variance: High. This is a hit-tool driven profile offensively, and we are a ways away from knowing if he can handle upper minors velocity, let alone major league stuff. If he does grow into a bit of pop—he's gotten some Brett Gardner comps—he could be…well, Brett Gardner I guess. But there's some risk he's just another slappy fourth outfielder type in three years. Which was also said about Brett Gardner as a prospect.

Mark Barry's Fantasy Take: If you're wondering where all the steals went, apparently they're all in this system. Carroll is going to steal a lot of bases. He's a little guy, so we still don't know if there will ever be any power, but if it comes, he could be a Lorenzo Cain-y-type guy.

6 | Brennan Malone   RHP   OFP: 60   ETA: 2022/23
Born: 09/08/00   Age: 19   Bats: R   Throws: R   Height: 6'4"   Weight: 205
Origin: Round 1C, 2019 Draft (#33 overall)

The Report: In the mix to be the first prep arm taken in this past year's draft, Malone fell into the compensation round as the fourth high school hurler taken. Given his mature, athletic body, repeatable mechanics, and advanced stuff for his age, it was a surprise he lasted as long as he did. Playing for one of the most prospect-laden teams we've seen in quite a while, he stood out as the go-to prospect on the squad.

He's able to locate his mid-90s fastball and does so early in games to set the tone. While the command isn't perfect, there is an effort to paint the corners and work all quadrants of the zone unlike a typical hard-thrower; there is moxy to his gameplan. Once the hitters attempt to speed up their bat, he's able to counter with a solid slider that works in the low 80s and has a sharp break to the glove-side. A decent 12-to-6 curveball is also employed, but it doesn't have the current ability to both land for strikes and chase swings like the slider does. There's even some feel for a changeup, but with such a solid foundation in all other parts of his game, it is the asset in need of most work.

Variance: Very high. Like any mature-bodied pitcher fresh out of high school, there is so much that can happen to a talented arm once it adjusts to a professional schedule.

Mark Barry's Fantasy Take: It's hard not to be intrigued by Malone's combination of a controllable slider and a fastball that flirts with triple digits. He's also a huge dude, and has a pair of developing secondaries that could firmly entrench him as a mid-rotation starter. He's also a pitching prospect, which as we all know can go horribly awry at a moment's notice. For now, let's call him rosterable in 200-prospect leagues.

7 Blake Walston LHP
OFP: 60 ETA: 2023/24
Born: 06/28/01 Age: 19 Bats: L Throws: L Height: 6'5" Weight: 175
Origin: Round 1, 2019 Draft (#26 overall)

The Report: Walston got picked a few spots ahead of Malone, and we prefer the surety of the latter at present, but it's a reasonably close call and could look very different after Walston gets a year of pro instruction. He's a tall, projectable lefty who's already touching 95 and flashes good sink and explosive life when he elevates armside. The combination of his quick arm and slingy three-quarters slot gets the fastball on you faster than you'd think low 90s would arrive. It might be mid 90s in time. There is a bit of upper body effort in the delivery at times, I'd expect that all to smooth out some as he fills out. Overall, it's a relatively clean delivery given his size.

Walston's secondaries are a bit raw, but there's some feel for a curveball that can show high spin and good 12-6 depth, although it does tend to flatten out and get slurvy at times. The changeup is rough, but it's a discernible changeup and advanced for a prep arm. He's confident throwing it in games, and can run it in to righties where it will flash some sink and fade, although he tends to guide and really cast it to turn it over. Walston is going to be a bit more of a project than Malone, but there's a smidge more upside if it all comes together.

Variance: Very high. Walston is just now focusing solely on baseball, and while the raw materials are all there, a lot has to go right for him to reach the projection. There's a decent reliever fallback as a fastball/curve lefty, but even that would be half a decade away.

Mark Barry's Fantasy Take: Walston is a fun guy to keep on the radar, and was arguably the best prep arm in the 2019 draft, but he's very, very far away, and you probably need around 250-300 prospects in your league for him to be rostered.

8. Corbin Martin   RHP
OFP: 55   **ETA:** 2019
Born: 12/28/95   Age: 24   Bats: R   Throws: R   Height: 6'2"   Weight: 200
Origin: Round 2, 2017 Draft (#56 overall)

The Report: Martin got off to a good start in the PCL, got bombed a bit in the Astros rotation, and then went down with a UCL tear. Shortly after surgery he was dealt to the Diamondbacks as part of the Zack Greinke trade. The stuff looked major-league-quality despite the command and long ball issues. Martin sits in the mid 90s and touched as high as 98. The fastball can run a little true but is explosive with "rise" when he elevates it. Both his slider and curve are potentially above-average, and while his change can be a bit firm, there's enough fade to make it a crossover option, even if it lacks the consistent tumble to miss bats. Will that all still be there eighteen months from now? How long will it take the command to come back? It's a cliche, but in this case literally only time will tell.

Variance: High. Well, I mean he's not likely to pitch again until 2021, and while Tommy John surgery is fairly common now, it's not by any means routine. Martin was major-league-ready with four average-or-better pitches, but until we see it back on the mound, there's going to be known unknowns here.

Mark Barry's Fantasy Take: Martin was fine in his five-start cup of coffee with the big club this season, but surrendered too many walks and dingers to be anything more than a fantasy SP6-7. Then he had Tommy John surgery, so we won't see him at all until 2021. Again, he's fine, but a preexisting lack of control doesn't bode well for his return to the bump. On a side note, there are way too many Corbins in this top 10.

9. Liover Peguero   SS
OFP: 60   **ETA:** 2023
Born: 12/31/00   Age: 19   Bats: R   Throws: R   Height: 6'1"   Weight: 160
Origin: International Free Agent, 2017

The Report: A mid-six figure bonus baby from the Diamondbacks' 2017 IFA class, Peguero is already paying dividends as a pro. It's one of the best frames to bet on out there—lean and strong, high-waisted and athletic, projectable, but not likely to grow off shortstop. It's the kind of body that my predecessor—who also happens to be the pro scouting director here—would gush over in these pages.

This isn't a mere projection bet on a Dominican teenager, though. Despite a little bit of an unorthodox swing—it's reminiscent of Jung-Ho Kang with his hands loaded out in front and a big leg kick—Peguero shows advanced barrel control for his age. Coupled with good wrists and explosive bat speed, there's potential for above-average hit and above-average power in the profile as he adds strength.

Peguero is a smooth shortstop and a plus runner at present. I'd expect him to bleed some of that speed as he fills out, but the frame is on the narrow side, and he's likely to stick and settle in at average or maybe a tick-above at the 6. The bat will carry the profile, but hey, it's a potentially special bat.

Variance: Extreme. He's an 18-year-old with a limited short-season resume.

Mark Barry's Fantasy Take: We talk a lot about getting in early on guys flashing loud tools in short-season league, and Peguero is one of the better examples of the type. He's a ways away, but he's above-average pretty much everywhere with the stick, and if he replicates his 2019 campaign, he absolutely won't be under the radar any longer.

10. Jon Duplantier   RHP

OFP: 55   ETA: 2019
Born: 07/11/94   Age: 25   Bats: L   Throws: R   Height: 6'4"   Weight: 225
Origin: Round 3, 2016 Draft (#89 overall)

The Report: Duplantier's durability concerns continue. After a bout of bicep tendinitis in 2018, shoulder inflammation cost him significant time in 2019. Those are two fairly concerning injuries for a pitching prospect, and the Diamondbacks used Duplantier solely in relief after his return to the big club in September. Honestly, he's not a bad fit there. He can lean on a power 12-6 curveball to miss bats and although his velocity dipped a bit this year into the low 90s, it's still a lively fastball with run. Duplantier offers a hard slider and serviceable change as well, but the command profile and delivery have always had strong bullpen markers, and while he has a full four-pitch mix, that may merely make him an option to go once through the lineup or so out of the pen. That's a useful arm though, assuming he can stay healthy.

Variance: Low. Duplantier is not without risks mind you, they are just known risks of the reliever and injury variety. He's major-league-ready.

Mark Barry's Fantasy Take: I would like Duplantier better if he struck out more guys, walked fewer and didn't get hurt so much. It's a bummer, and probably a little reductive, but his is a profile that's hard to bet on long-term.

The Next Ten

11. J.B. Bukauskas   RHP

Born: 10/11/96   Age: 23   Bats: R   Throws: R   Height: 6'0"   Weight: 196
Origin: Round 1, 2017 Draft (#15 overall)

In the 2019 Annual, Bukauskas' blurb posited that if he "can just stay healthy and throw strikes, he's one of the few pitchers in the minors with top-of-the-rotation potential." He promptly missed a chunk of the season with elbow soreness and walked 14 percent of batters when he was on the mound. The stuff is still tantalizing enough that he was a key piece of the Diamondbacks' return for Zack Greinke, but his future looks more like that of a key bullpen piece now. Bukauskas remains a short, physically maxed righty with a potential plus fastball/slider combo. The fastball is lively, but sits in more of an average velocity band when he's stretched out, although it's mid 90s in short bursts. The slider is a true out pitch, firm with late dive. There's a cutter and a serviceable change as well, so like Duplantier, you can squint and see a rotation piece, but also like Duplantier, the consistent command and injury issues as a pro make late-inning relief the likely outcome.

12 Blaze Alexander SS
Born: 06/11/99 Age: 21 Bats: R Throws: R Height: 6'0" Weight: 160
Origin: Round 11, 2018 Draft (#339 overall)

Short but with a medium frame, Alexander is a pure athlete with plus body control. His solid footwork and quick-twitch movements stand out—especially in the field, where he is strongest. He has the ability to play shortstop, second and third base at premium levels, though he primarily profiles as an up-the-middle type player. Working around the bag at second, Alexander shows impressive instincts, reads and fundamentals. His hands are quick and smooth, which match his swift footwork. But Alexander's arm strength and accuracy are the most impressive part of his game. There aren't many guys in the minors that showcase the amount of carry on throws as Alexander does. In the box is where the question marks begin. Overall, he has slightly above-average bat to ball skills and a short swing with small uppercut, but his pitch selection needs refinement. There also is not much, if any, power in the tank. And with his frame I don't see him ever hitting for power. Alexander has above-average wheels and knows how to swipe a bag. The profile fits as a defensive specialist.

13 Seth Beer OF
Born: 09/18/96 Age: 23 Bats: L Throws: R Height: 6'3" Weight: 195
Origin: Round 1, 2018 Draft (#28 overall)

Once upon a time, Beer was considered to be a lock to go first overall in the 2018 draft. He had a strong junior campaign in a tough conference, but his slide down the draft board started the previous fall and went through the spring, eventually landing him with the Astros at pick 28. There's obvious limitations to the profile. Beer is unathletic at both corner outfield and first base. While he's not a complete zero there, he's comfortably below-average and best suited to DH.

You'd be expecting a long and strong power profile at the plate based on the above, and there's some truth to that. Beer only has average bat speed and it's not a true launch angle uppercut, but he's strong enough to muscle balls out to the pull side and he's a better pure hitter than you'd think. He has good barrel control despite the stiff swing, and a strong approach at the plate. He can get pull-happy, leading to swing-and-miss in the zone, especially against offspeed, but as three true outcome sluggers go, Beer is a better bet to hit .270 or .280 than most. That might not be enough to make him more than a second-division corner bat, but he's hit everywhere so far, and the PCL isn't likely to offer him much more of a challenge.

14 Wilderd Patino   OF
Born: 07/18/01   Age: 18   Bats: R   Throws: R   Height: 6'1"   Weight: 175
Origin: International Free Agent, 2017

Patino is even more of a physical freak than Liover Peguero, although the overall game is much rawer. Patino is a pure burner on the bases and in center field, with plus speed he can get to quickly and enough present feel on the grass to project a plus center fielder at maturity. At the plate, it's raw, with an aggressive approach and some issues with pitch recognition. There's also good hand speed and a projectable frame. Like with Peguero, the wrists just work. Patino tends to think he's more of a power hitter than he is at present and swings like it. But there's some room to fill out and get stronger in his upper body at least, so fringe pop might come, rounding out the profile and making him a top-of-the-order weapon.

15 Levi Kelly   RHP
Born: 05/14/99   Age: 21   Bats: R   Throws: R   Height: 6'4"   Weight: 205
Origin: Round 8, 2018 Draft (#249 overall)

In his first full-season assignment, Kelly turned himself from a probable future bullpen arm to a potential rotation piece. The delivery was simplified and overall control cleaned up by a transition to working out of the stretch exclusively. He also took a big step with the development of his secondaries, most notably the slider. He has confidence in it and it is a true weapon, showing two-plane movement and fading away from right-handed hitters. It plays well off of the fastball which sits in the mid 90s and has some late life. That fastball/slider combination gives Kelly a solid floor of a late-inning reliever. However, he was unhittable at times last year and if another secondary develops he'll solidify his role as a starter.

16 Drey Jameson   RHP
Born: 08/17/97   Age: 22   Bats: R   Throws: R   Height: 6'0"   Weight: 165
Origin: Round 1C, 2019 Draft (#34 overall)

After a dominant sophomore season at Ball State, the draft-eligible Jameson became yet another first-round pick for Arizona. He's an undersized righty—listed at 6-foot, 165 pounds—with an uptempo, effortful delivery, so there's strong reliever risk here. His fastball sat comfortably in the mid 90s when starting, though, and there may be more in short bursts. He pairs the fastball with a tight 12-6 curve which gives him the second pitch for late-inning work. There's a hard slider and a changeup—both potentially average—as well, but the mechanics, size, and overall command profile might limit him to late-inning pen work.

17 Luis Frias   RHP
Born: 05/23/98   Age: 22   Bats: R   Throws: R   Height: 6'3"   Weight: 180
Origin: International Free Agent, 2015

Originally signed as a third baseman in 2015 out of the Dominican Republic, the D'Backs moved the extra-large-framed but athletic Frias to the mound a year later. So far, the move has paid off as he fanned 101 batters over 76 1/3 innings between short-season and Low-A. Frias is in the conversation for the most electric stuff in Arizona's system. His four-pitch mix offers two potential plus pitches. Frias' straight fastball sits mid 90s and can touch 98 mph. He creates a steep downhill plane with it as he throws almost straight over the top. At times fastball command can be elusive when he overthrows, but overall control isn't an issue. Frias' best pitch is his 12-6 hammer curveball—one of the best I saw all year. Thrown in the low 80s, it has sharp, late bite and plenty of depth to it. He shows plus command of the breaker, throwing it for strikes or inducing chases and hitters from both sides of the plate look flabbergasted when trying to attack it. Frias also offers a mid-80s slider that has inconsistent shape but showed solid horizontal movement, and a high-80s split-changeup with hard tumble. Better feel and command for both of these secondaries is needed, but his split-changeup has a chance to be another big whiff pitch. With two plus swing-and-miss pitches, Frias has a solid floor as a relief arm and an intriguingly high ceiling if the rest of the arsenal rounds out with more mound experience.

18 Tommy Henry LHP
Born: 07/29/97   Age: 22   Bats: L   Throws: L   Height: 6'3"   Weight: 205
Origin: Round 2, 2019 Draft (#74 overall)

Another 2019 draft pick to cover. Unlike the other new arms in the system, Henry is more of a polish guy than a stuff guy. A typical good college lefty in a lot of ways, he mixes a low-90s fastball in with an above-average changeup with solid dive and a short and slurvy slider that he commands well. It's a solid starter's frame, and Henry might even have a smidge of projection left despite being on the older side for a college pick. He was used heavily at Michigan during their College World Series run, so he only made a few one-inning appearances as a pro. We'll have more info on whether or not his command of averageish stuff plays against pro hitters next year, but for now he looks like your typical OFP 50 / No. 4 starter type, which is impressive to still be finding this deep in a system list.

19 Dominic Fletcher OF
Born: 09/02/97   Age: 22   Bats: L   Throws: L   Height: 5'9"   Weight: 185
Origin: Round 2, 2019 Draft (#75 overall)

David Fletcher's younger brother was drafted out of Arkansas in 2019's Competitive Balance Round. Fletcher, Dominic that is, has an extra-large frame with thick, strong legs. The D'Backs pushed him to High-A Kane County and he was not overmatched. At the plate Fletcher controls the zone well with above-average plate coverage, displaying plus barrel control most of the time. He can spray it line-to-line, making him more of a contact guy than a true home run threat, but he has above-average raw power; his ability to transfer that power into games is still up for debate. Fletcher's swing is reminiscent of Brett Gardner's. He uses a lot of his upper half and doesn't engage his lower half fully, resulting in a long swing on occasion, especially on pitches up in the zone. Fletcher's slightly above-average speed should make him a marginal stolen base threat. Defensively, he can play all three outfield spots. The 5-foot-9, 185-pounder moves with ease and swiftness, showing fluid movements and routes—a plus defender. His arm flashes plus at times but sits comfortably in the above-average range. Fletcher is a grinder, and profiles as an average, everyday center fielder with a floor as a platoon outfielder.

20 Andy Young IF
Born: 05/10/94 Age: 26 Bats: R Throws: R Height: 6'0" Weight: 195
Origin: Round 37, 2016 Draft (#1126 overall)

The other, other part of the Paul Goldschmidt deal, there was plenty of residual Cardinals Devil Magic left in the former 37th-round small college infielder. There might not be a prospect who enjoyed the new PCL ball more than Young, who smashed 21 home runs in just 68 games for Reno. That overstates his power projection, but there's solid raw with some feel to hit. The plate approach and glove are limiting factors here and probably make Young more of a useful bench piece than an everyday guy, but he can stand at a bunch of infield spots and is a potentially better-than-average bat. Those guys tend to get 300 PA here and there for a while.

Personal Cheeseball

PC Domingo Leyba 2B
Born: 09/11/95 Age: 24 Bats: B Throws: R Height: 5'11" Weight: 160
Origin: International Free Agent, 2006

Arizona Diamondbacks 2020

Man, I really wanted to get Leyba on this list. It's just too deep and laden with upside to justify it. I still think he can be a second-division starter at the keystone, and at worst he's a useful extra infielder with a broad base of skills. Mostly he's a link back to when this system wasn't, uh, quite this good and he was top-five, but at least a little interesting to write about. Now the system is far more up my alley, loaded with interesting prep arms, and high-waisted teenaged athlete bats. Leyba is extremely neither of those, a 24-year-old middle infielder who's stretched at short, not particularly athletic, and missed chunks of 2017 and 2018 while the system improved around him. He can hit a bit though, and while he's likely squeezed out of a clear 2020 role with Arizona despite a solid September cameo, Leyba is clearly the system's cheeseball.

Low Minors Sleeper

LMS

Jeferson Espinal   OF
Born: 06/07/02   Age: 18   Bats: L   Throws: L   Height: 6'0"   Weight: 180
Origin: International Free Agent, 2018

We leave my favorite (not best, Rays fans, calm down) system with one more toolsy teenager for the road. Espinal is a lesser version of Patino at present although he carries a similar center field profile. He's more likely to project as the bench outfielder version, as he lacks some of Patino's physicality, and may be more of a slash and burn guy. Check back in two years, though by then I am sure all your dynasty league mates will have rostered him due to his Northwest League steal totals.

Top Talents 25 and Under (as of 4/1/2020)

1. Kristian Robinson
2. Carson Kelly
3. Zac Gallen
4. Alek Thomas
5. Daulton Varsho
6. Geraldo Perdomo
7. Corbin Carroll
8. Brennan Malone
9. Blake Walston
10. Corbin Martin

There are few talents in baseball, let alone inside the Diamondbacks' organization, that boast the kind of impact talent that Kristian Robinson is capable of deploying at peak. He's got plus-plus physicality that looks more applicable to a college football field more than a baseball diamond. But he has a good idea of what he's doing with both the bat and the glove and if he can get to most of his projection, he's going to be a very good one. If he gets to all of it, well, let's not go there just yet because he just turned 19.

Carson Kelly's ability to catch has never been in question, but he used 2019 to prove that all of those forecasts about his hitting weren't in vain. He ate lefties for lunch but had a much tougher time against arm-side pitching. He's still a tremendous asset who's already proven his worth. And, given his lack of consistent big league experience, may have yet another gear to grab. Zac Gallen came to Arizona mid-season in a swap for Jazz Chisholm and immediately looked the part of a controllable mid-rotation starter. There isn't one particular carrying tool or pitch in his arsenal that jumps off the page. The changeup is the best of the bunch, however, and the control is there for him to keep up this kind of profile with a chance to take another step forward.

Alek Thomas has pushed himself into comfortable top-100 territory with his monster 2019 campaign. An advanced approach has served him well and there's enough physical strength in his compact frame to allow for more pop to come than might meet the eye at first glance. Staying in center field would help his stock, but he could also be a real asset in left should it come to that down the line. You're probably well aware that Daulton Varsho can hit. Where he lines up remains the question. An electronic strike zone could allow him to stay behind the dish, but he should be able to slide into left field easily enough or even, perhaps, take some reps at second if he doesn't catch much. A super-utility guy with his hitting ability should allow Torey Lovullo to get creative on a nightly basis.

Geraldo Perdomo popped up in the summer of 2018 then impressed that fall. Since then, he has performed well in full season ball, High-A and the Arizona Fall League (almost all of that production came at the age of 19, by the way). Corbin Carroll made his presence felt immediately after being drafted and has a chance to wind up the best outfielder in this system, depending on how he and his soon-to-be teammates mature. Brennan Malone was a luxury with the 33rd overall pick in June, thanks in part to all of those draft picks, and has plenty of upside. Arizona was all over Walston pre-draft and popped him 26th overall. The lanky lefty didn't pitch much in his debut but is a player development bet with a high rate of return should he pay off. Corbin Martin joined the organization in the Greinke deal and, despite his ongoing TJ rehab, should be a solid asset for the D-backs long-term.

The Diamondbacks' big league squad is intriguing in how age is currently distributed across the roster. Arizona should feature a bunch of guys playing in their age-26 through age-31 seasons. That's to say, the team won't be especially young, but not especially old, either. As the list above shows, however, there's another wave on the way. While the D-backs intend to compete in 2020, there

Arizona Diamondbacks 2020

should be plenty of rolling turnover in the next few years as these prospects matriculate to the majors. The Diamondbacks' roster should get collectively younger in the process, but that's still a year or two off.

Part 3: Featured Articles

The Baseball Is Juiced (Again)

Robert Arthur

This article originally appeared at Baseball Prospectus on April 5, 2019.

It started when the normally reliable Chris Sale got lit up for three homers by the Mariners in the Red Sox's season opener. It was part of a record number of taters that flew on Opening Day, as starters from Sale to Zack Greinke were taken deep by the handful. Then Christian Yelich hit a home run in each of his first four games, tying yet another MLB record, this one for consecutive games with a dinger to start a season.

It didn't take long for fans and players to begin whispering and tweeting about the baseballs being juiced again. It's early yet for us to come to any definitive conclusion about the 2019 season, but preliminary data shows that the baseball has returned to its aerodynamic peak. Whether that means this season will smash home run records like 2017 did remains to be seen.

Before home run explosion over the last few years, no one worried too much about the baseball's air resistance. While MLB and Rawlings (the company that manufactures the official baseballs) kept track of dozens of metrics to make sure that the ball was consistent from month to month, they didn't measure drag.

But drag is incredibly important in determining how likely a hitter is to knock one out of the park. As baseballs become more aerodynamic, they travel further given a certain initial velocity. A deep fly ball that might have been caught at the warning track can instead go into the first row of the stands. A three percent change in drag coefficient can work to add about five feet to a well-hit fly ball, which can in turn increase home runs league wide by an astounding 10-15 percent.

It's possible to measure the aerodynamics of the baseball using the pitch-tracking radars currently in place in each MLB ballpark. By calculating the loss of speed from when the pitch is released to when it crosses the plate, you can directly measure the drag coefficient on the baseball. I first wrote about the role of decreasing drag in boosting home runs in 2017, and MLB's commission of scientists and statisticians later confirmed that the more aerodynamic baseballs in use that year were largely to blame for the spike in home runs. The same commission rejected some alternate hypotheses, like rising temperatures and a league-wide boost in launch angle pushing more balls over the fence.

The current era has featured some large fluctuations in drag coefficient, leading to first an explosion in 2016 and 2017, and then a dialing back of homers last year. Curious about the record-breaking home run tallies in the last few days, I used the same methodology to measure the aerodynamics of the baseballs so far in 2019.

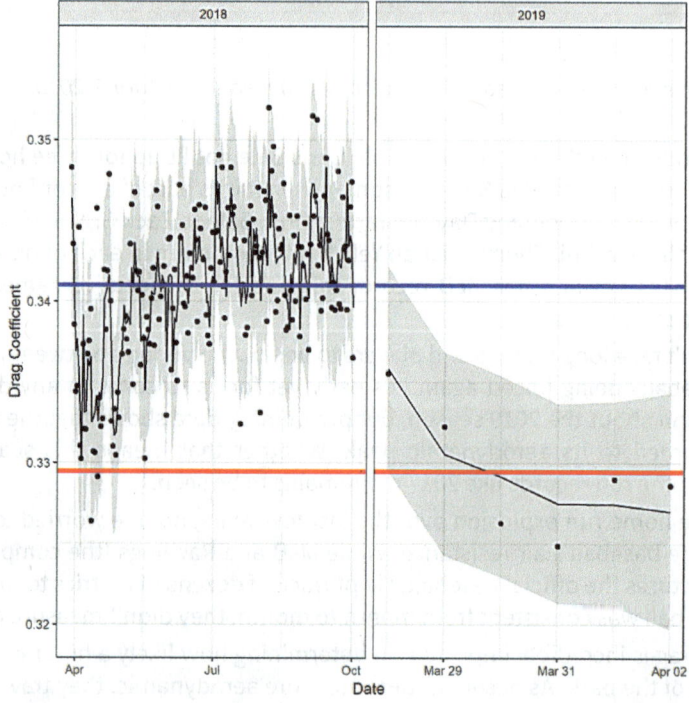

We're only a week into the 2019 season, but the drag numbers so far are among the lowest recorded in the last calendar year. With apologies for gory math, the current 2019 season average drag coefficient (the red line) would be below the 95 percent credible interval (the shaded area) for about nine-tenths of the 2018 season. (I used a Bayesian Random Walk model implemented in INLA to calculate these credible intervals, averaging the drag numbers in each game and adjusting for park.)

There were only a handful of six-day stretches in 2018 that had drag numbers below what we're seeing now, and most were in late June and early July. All of this means that 2019's data so far is quite a bit different than what we saw through most of last year.

These drag coefficients factor out the effects of temperature and air density, so they aren't a product of April cold. However, the numbers could be deceptive if the radars used to track pitches have changed from year to year. I consulted with some experts within baseball who were not aware of any specific modifications to the radar this year that could produce this pattern, but it's an important caveat of which to be aware.

On the one hand, it's only been six days, and we don't quite have the statistical basis to say that these drag coefficients are unprecedented compared to 2018. On the other hand, we've witnessed about 5,000 fastballs so far this season, so it's not as if our sample size is small. At least so far, the baseball has played like it's much more aerodynamic than it was last year. In fact, the current drag coefficient is really only comparable to 2017, when the baseballs were more aerodynamic than they had been in at least a decade.

It's not just fancy radar tracking indicating that the baseball is flying through the air more easily. The current number of home runs per game (as of this writing) is the highest it's been since the heady days of 2017, the year that teams and players broke dinger-related records everywhere you looked. That's especially remarkable considering that we're in what is typically the coldest part of the regular season, when lower temperatures and higher winds tend to suppress offense and keep balls in the air within the park. Comparing only from April to April, this year's rate of home runs per fly ball is even a little bit higher than it was in 2017.

With that said, the current measurements are no guarantee that 2019 will be another year of record-shattering homer hitting. The trouble with the drag measurements is that they are not consistent from June to August, from week to week, or even sometimes from day to day. Whether because of natural manufacturing variation or differences in the underlying supplies of cowhide and thread that go into the baseballs, drag has a tendency to fluctuate up and down over the course of a year. So the homers that fly in the first week of April wouldn't necessarily clear the fence a week later.

It's possible that this one-week drop in drag coefficient subsides and the baseball returns to its 2018 levels. On the other hand, it's almost equally probable that the ball becomes even more slippery and flies ever farther. Either way, it's clear that the baseball's air resistance is something to keep an eye on for the remainder of the 2019 season.

—*Robert Arthur is an author of Baseball Prospectus.*

The Moral Hazard of Playing It Safe

Craig Goldstein

This article originally appeared at Baseball Prospectus on August 6, 2019.

A couple days prior to the trade deadline, amidst a sea of tranquility posing as the lead up to the trade deadline, Bob Nightengale took to Twitter. Nightengale, who was probably wearing his pants backwards at the time, tweeted that MLB GMs were coming around on the idea that the unified trade deadline should be moved back from July 31 to August 15, so they could better assess their positions in the standings and whether they should buy or sell. To which I said:

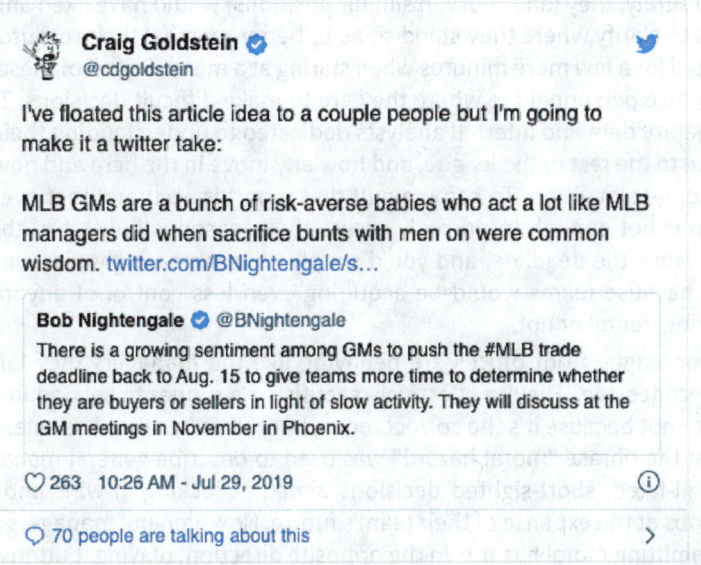

This might strike some as reductive and churlish. And it might be that, but it isn't really wrong, either. Jeff Quinton wrote a great piece discussing the environmental factors that enable front offices to avoid risk without upsetting the apple cart within their own fanbases. I don't believe that it goes far enough, however. His article gives us the proper framework through which to understand why these behaviors have been allowed to seep into front offices throughout the league. Understanding the reasons behind these actions are different from excusing them, though, and GMs should not be let off the hook for their non-competitive approach to the trade deadline (much less the offseason).

⚾ ⚾ ⚾

It's fair to say that fans as a group have rarely, if ever, been pro-player. It is also fair to say that in the time during and following the Moneyball revolution, the pendulum swung from fans who cared intensely about winning in the moment (and thus might be intolerant of a rebuilding approach) to fans who supported building a team that could compete throughout multiple seasons, viewing the playoffs as a crapshoot, with the thought that getting multiple bites at the apple was a better approach than taking a bigger bite in any one season.

There's nothing wrong with that approach, and I still find merit in that argument. However, it seems that the pendulum has swung too far in that direction. Teams are overvaluing some of the individual factors that make themselves long-term contenders rather than attempting to seize a championship when given the opportunity. It's a difficult needle to thread.

And surely, they (and those in similar positions) would have liked another two weeks to clarify where they stand so as to better marshal their resources. We've all asked for a few more minutes when staring at a menu. But all of these GMs and front office personnel are where they are to make difficult decisions. They have proprietary data and internal analysts dedicated to understanding their position relative to the rest of the league, and how any move in the here and now impacts their long-term vision. To complain (if that report is accurate) that over half the season is not enough to properly assess their season is bullshit of the highest order. Move the deadline, and you'd simply have increasingly discounted trade offers because teams would be acquiring even less control of anyone they're acquiring, rental or not.

Major league front offices are behaving like the managers they lampooned two decades ago. They're effectively sacrificing a runner to second in the ninth inning—not because it's the correct move, but rather because it is safe. It used to be that the phrase "moral hazard" was used to describe general managers who made ill-fated, short-sighted decisions aimed at locking in wins and securing their jobs at the expense of their team's future. Now, general managers are guilty of committing moral hazards in the opposite direction, playing it utterly safe and terrified of becoming scapegoats.

In lieu of bold action, they opt to pussyfoot around a current window of contention, choosing instead to play the long game and stack up years of control like they're blocks in a game of Jenga. GMs pass on signing quality players in free agency because the back-end of the deal might look bad, and because they might be able to squeeze out 70 percent of the production from a player who costs a tenth as much. That's a safer investment, too, because it's also hard to prove a negative—it's impossible to prove that Manny Machado would make the Mets a playoff team in 2019-2020, but it's easy to say that the back half of Robinson Cano's contract sucks. Owners, who rule over GM's jobs, are also humans with human brain processes that will always make the so-called albatross contract uglier than the road not taken.

These days, GMs are remembered for the bad deals they make and the surplus value they generate, not the acquisition of expensive, necessary talents that meet their market worth (or fall slightly short while still providing significant on-field value). And front offices know that one or two expensive misfires can cost them their jobs, no matter how many good deals they make.

No front office exemplifies this ethos more than the Toronto Blue Jays. General Manager Ross Atkins had this to say following the Blue Jays underwhelming trade deadline:

This is by no means the first time that an executive will cite years of control to justify their actions, which is often just another way of saying "don't look at what we got, look at how much we got of it." Atkins touts quantity to elide the discussion of quality—either, that of the players acquired, or those given up. Remember: the other teams presumably value years of control, too.

Atkins also had some thoughts to offer regarding free agents back in early 2018:

This ignores, of course, whether the player can create enough value in the front end of a contract to justify the longer term of a deal, and the decline that often occurs in the back end. It also ignores whether the player can fill a need the team requires and put them in a position to compete for and win a championship. But as teams seemingly avoid contention at all, where they might end up having to consider and later justify some of these tough decisions, we still see risk-averse approaches.

Anthony Fenech's article on two trades that recently extended GM Al Avila didn't make got at this issue rather well:

> Passing on those deals was defensible: Both players had yet to break out and trading [Michael] Fulmer—a pitcher who appeared to be a future ace, no matter his injury concerns—would have taken serious gumption, opening Avila up to strong criticism.

Avoiding strong criticism is something each of us can understand as a motivation, but the avoidance of criticism only matters if that criticism is valid. In Fulmer's case, shoving his injury concerns aside affects not only the years that the team controls him (he is currently missing a full season due to Tommy John surgery) but also the quality of those seasons, as his knee and elbow injuries combined to dampen his effectiveness even when healthy enough to pitch. But it was easy to present the then-current image of Fulmer as a top of the rotation pitcher who the team had under its domain for the next five seasons as something to build around. The status quo isn't nearly as often second-guessed as a decision that disrupts it.

⚾ ⚾ ⚾

MLB GMs are risk-averse to a fault. They are ivy-educated and consulting firm-approved, and yet they can't seem to avoid leaving wins on the table in their all-consuming lust for a non-existent $/WAR championship. They are supposed to zig when everyone else zags, and not merely pay lip service to the idea of zigging through a calculated PR plan built on convincing the fan base their approach is novel when it actually apes most of their competitors. Instead they've become far more concerned with making safe, accepted-by-the-new-common-wisdom decisions, such that our prior understanding of what a moral hazard is has become inverted.

I can't blame them entirely, and not only because of the reasons that Quinton illuminated in his article, but also because of the damage wrought by the introduction of the second wild card (WC2) spot. MLB's desire to have more teams in playoff contention has sparked anti-competitive behavior. Teams know now that they do not need to swing big as they assemble their roster because there is a good chance that a mediocre team can either catch fire and capture a division, or muddle along until they back into the WC2.

Simultaneously, the one-game playoff has neutered the WC1, putting an entire season on the flip of a coin like some sort of baseball-obsessed Anton Chigurh. While the one-game playoff makes sense as a way to increase the value of winning a division, it also means that if a front office doesn't like its chances of overcoming a behemoth like the Dodgers or Astros in the offseason, they have few incentives to chase glory. Similarly, the relative inaction in the NL Central at the trade deadline—despite a wide open division—can be explained by the idea that any high-variance investment could still result in only a wild card (or worse) result, given the mere two months left in the season to make an impact.

⚾ ⚾ ⚾

As stated at the top, we should not confuse reasons for excuses. The implementation of the second wild card is just one of many environmental factors that influence how each front office operates. I am convinced that it is one of the larger factors, but I am also convinced that organizations need to shed the yoke of "efficiency at all costs" so that they can instead pursue competition, as the spirit of the game intends. Until they do, we're all deadline losers.

—*Craig Goldstein is an author of Baseball Prospectus.*

Index of Names

Ahmed, Nick 20
Alexander, Blaze 96, 108
Almonte, Abraham 96
Barrosa, Jorge 96
Beer, Seth 86, 108
Bradley, Archie 54
Bukauskas, J.B. 93, 107
Bumgarner, Madison 56
Calhoun, Kole 22
Carroll, Corbin 96, 104
Chafin, Andrew 58
Clarke, Taylor 98
Crichton, Stefan 98
Cron, Kevin 96
Duplantier, Jon 60, 107
English, Tristin 96
Escobar, Eduardo 24
Espinal, Jeferson 96, 112
Fletcher, Dominic 96, 110
Frias, Luis 98, 109
Gallen, Zac 62
Ginkel, Kevin 64
Grace, Matt 66
Green, Josh 98
Guerra, Junior 68
Henry, Tommy 110
Hicks, John 26
Hill, Glenallen 96
Holland, Greg 98
Jackson, Edwin 70
Jameson, Drey 98, 109
Jay, Jon 28
Jones, Adam 30
Joseph, Caleb 96
Kelly, Carson 32
Kelly, Levi 98, 109
Kelly, Merrill 72
Koch, Matthew 98
Lamb, Jake 34
Leake, Mike 74
Leyba, Domingo 96, 111
Locastro, Tim 36
Lopez, Yoan 98
Malone, Brennan 98, 104
Marte, Ketel 38
Marte, Starling 40
Martin, Corbin 76, 106
Mathisen, Wyatt 96
McCarthy, Jake 87
Nelson, Ryne 98
Patino, Wilderd 96, 109
Payamps, Joel 98
Peguero, Liover 106
Peralta, David 42
Perdomo, Geraldo 44, 103
Ray, Robbie 78
Robinson, Kristian 88, 101
Rojas, Josh 46
Rondón, Héctor 80
Scott, Robby 98
Sherfy, Jimmie 98
Smith, Pavin 89

Arizona Diamondbacks 2020

Smith, Riley 98
Tabor, Matt 98
Takahashi, Bo 94
Thomas, Alek 90, 102
Tomás, Yasmany 91
Vargas, Emilio 98
Vargas, Ildemaro 48
Varsho, Daulton 92, 102
Vogt, Stephen 50
Walker, Christian 52
Walston, Blake 98, 105
Weaver, Luke 82
Widener, Taylor 95
Yerzy, Andy 96
Young, Alex 84
Young, Andy 96, 111